THE BOOK OF QUEER MORMON JOY

THE
BOOK
OF
QUEER
MORMON
JOY

EDITED BY
KERRY SPENCER PRAY

SIGNATURE BOOKS | 2024 | SALT LAKE CITY

Join our mail list at www.signaturebooks.com for details on events and related titles we think you'll enjoy.

Design by Jason Francis

FIRST EDITION | 2024

LIBRARY OF CONGRESS CONTROL NUMBER: 2024935100

Paperback ISBN: 978-1-56085-470-8
Ebook ISBN: 978-1-56085-488-3

CONTENTS

SECTION 2: JOY IS DEFIANCE AND FAITH

SECTION 3: JOY IS GRATITUDE FOR HOME

FOREWORD

CAROL LYNN PEARSON

Over sixty years ago, when life first introduced me to the subject of "queerness," the idea of coupling that word with "joy" was impossible. I rejoice that today very few people who pick up this book will find it shocking to read the title and am grateful to the people who helped make it possible.

My own experience started in 1966 when I married a gay man in the Salt Lake Mormon temple. Gerald had confided in me some past gay indiscretions, but we had both been assured by our church authorities that repentance and marriage to a good woman was the answer.

We had a good marriage in so many important ways, even joyful ways. And I owe my career as a writer to this man. In the second year of our marriage he insisted on our self-publishing my first book, a slim collection of poems titled *Beginnings.* By some strange twist of fortune, that book instantly put me on the map in Mormondom and opened the door to everything I have since accomplished. Even the general authorities quoted me. Who but a dear, queer husband would even entertain the idea of publishing his wife's poems?

After twelve years and four children and tremendous love mixed with anguish, we learned that someone's sexual orientation is not to be changed by personal determination or by a variety of "cures." We decided to end the marriage and remain good friends. Six years later, in 1984, Gerald passed away from AIDS in my home where I was taking care of him.

Knowing that our experience could be useful to so many, I determined to write our story. *Goodbye, I Love You* was published by Random House in 1986. This became a major media event not only in Mormondom, but nationally.

Since that time I have watched with awe and gratitude the groundswell of change in our national perception of the LGBTQ members of our human family. Our gay, trans, and queer siblings have taught us so much. Our progress has not been smooth and it is not complete, but it has been a remarkable thing to watch, and for me to continue to participate in.

Still, history moves more slowly than we'd like. In 2007 I published *No More Goodbyes: Circling the Wagons around Our Gay Loved Ones.* The book told true stories of many LDS gay men and women who had taken their own lives or attempted to—or who had lost relationships with their families—or who had suffered the heart-breaking consequences of entering into an ill-fated traditional marriage.

And then in 2008 came the debacle of Proposition 8 banning same-sex marriage in California, truly a joyless event. Generally—and certainly within Mormondom—that event seemed to powerfully activate LGBTQ people and their allies—as well as, of course, their enemies. (And yes, out on my front yard was a sign that read, "NO ON 8.")

And there was my friend Brad, who wept as he told me how much he loved the church and of his suicide attempt because he believed he would forever be unworthy of the joy of being able to love and be loved. He told of one night going to the site of the Provo Temple—"because there would be kind spirits there to help me over," and took a lethal dose of pills. The next morning he was found unconscious in a field and was in a coma for two weeks. Brad and I became close friends and his unnecessary pain is seared into my heart.

Proposition 8 was declared illegal in 2010. But then in 2015 came The "exclusion policy," another joyless event, making it mandatory that LDS gay couples be disciplined for apostasy and their children refused baptism until they were eighteen and disavowed same-sex relationships. Four years later—without explanation—that policy was withdrawn.

Yes, history moves slowly. But it does move. On the subject we speak of here, I am amazed at the changes that I have personally witnessed over the last fifty years. We are now at a place in our country—and even in our church—in which a majority of us acknowledge LGBTQ people as full citizens, as beautiful contributors to society, as good friends and associates, as our neighbors, our siblings, our children. And as the loved children of our Mother/Father in Heaven.

Indeed, we are at a place in history in which we can hear queer people tell their own stories, and we believe them, knowing that—like everyone else in the human family—our gay, trans, and queer members "are indeed that they might have joy!"

INTRODUCTION
THE JOY OF DANCING:
THE LIVES OF MODERN
LGBTQ MORMONS

ROBERT A. REES

Having been an active ally of LGBTQ individuals in the Latter-day Saint Church and Mormon community for the past half century, I was intrigued, enlightened, and inspired by the personal stories in this collection. *Intrigued*, because I was fascinated anew by the mysterious richness and complexity of human sexual and gender diversity; *enlightened*, because as much as I felt or thought I knew about the variety and complexity of the orientations and identities associated with this community, I now understand much more; *inspired*, because the courage, faith, and love these personal stories reveal have broadened my mind, expanded my soul and greatly enlarged my heart.

But I have also been *saddened* because of the rejection, hostility, abandonment, and abuse that most of the writers experienced in their families and religious communities as they grappled with what it is like to have been born with a sexual orientation and/or gender identity that is radically at odds with the expected norms of their social and religious communities.

Kerry Spencer Pray is to be congratulated for finding such a rich array of individual voices from across the LGBTQ spectrum and within the Latter-day Saint/Mormon community, and then helping them shape their personal stories into compelling narratives. Along with the related anthology, *I Spoke to You with Silence: Essays from Queer Mormons of Marginalized Genders* (University of Utah Press,

2022), edited by Pray and Jenn Lee Smith, this collection gives voice to a community whose voices traditionally have been silenced, ignored, or punished—much to their disadvantage and, I believe, much to the detriment of the LDS community of which they have been or still are a part.

One of the inspiring themes of this book is found in the metaphor of dancing, since neither dancing nor joy has been characteristic of the lives of LGBTQ individuals within the Mormon community over the past seventy years. Such individuals have had to face the challenge of either being unseen or seen as having deliberately chosen lifestyles that are considered perverse, willfully rebellious, and sinful according to the clearly established norms of their religious and civil societies. Martha Graham calls dance "the hidden language of the soul." The stories in this book reveal that hidden language in powerful ways.

When Pray, the collection's editor, refers to "dancing in the dim light," she is being both optimistic and realistic. The "dim light"—a reference from the gnostic gospel of John—provides an apt description of the challenge LGBTQ Mormons face. That such a thing as dancing is even possible for members of this community is a fact of radical hope. The dim light in which they dance might be like "the first gleam of dawn, which shines ever brighter until the full light of day" (Proverbs 4:18). The realization of that "full light" is dependent on the extent to which families, friends, church leaders, and members accept and welcome those who heretofore have not been welcomed or accepted, let alone celebrated. Based on my experience, neither dancing nor joy has been abundant for those who constitute this queer Mormon community.

Dancing is a whole body, whole soul experience that, almost invariably, is associated with joy. "You dance love and you dance joy and you dance dreams," said Gene Kelly. Pray states that she deliberately chose joy as a focus because "I couldn't handle putting together another book that told the *whole* truth about what it means to be a queer Mormon. Because the whole truth is gut-wrenching. Knowing the whole truth is too much, even for me, who lived it. It's all so heavy." That heaviness is attributable to the fact that, since the mid-twentieth century, the Latter-day Saint Church and community have failed to understand that a small but significant group of its members have had to contend with a complex set of personal, social, political, relational, and spiritual challenges with regard to their sexual orientation and/or gender identity that are at odds with their religious community.

Having worked within this community for decades, I can attest that it has been characterized much more by anguish of spirit and heaviness of heart than by dancing and joy. Nevertheless, as this collection of personal essays bears witness, the narrative is shifting, however reluctantly and slowly, toward enlightenment and acceptance—and we can be grateful to Pray and the authors she has selected for having the courage to tell their stories and the resilience to find joy in the telling.

The complex nature of that joy is honored in the structure of this collection. The stories are arranged into three categories: "Joy Is Complicated," "Joy Is Defiance and Faith," and "Joy Is Gratitude for Home," each of which is introduced by elements of Pray's own personal experiences as a queer woman negotiating the complex and frequently fraught territory of Mormon family, church, and society.

Pray asks the question at the beginning of her first section, "What do you think it means to have joy?" She confesses that "Joy is a complicated emotion." This collection is a sort of compendium on that complication or, more accurately, those complications.

Although the Book of Mormon states declaratively that we were created to experience joy, it also teaches that such joy is often dependent on sorrow, pain, and disappointment that there must be opposition in all things (2 Nephi 2:11). We are also taught that we can't know (and enjoy) the sweet without tasting the bitter (D&C 29:39). Or as Pray puts it, "Joy isn't joy unless it's ... earned. It's defiant. It comes *after* pain. *After* struggle. It's the feeling of finally finding freedom when you have only ever been imprisoned." That is why joy is palpable in so many of these stories. We now need to match that insight and intelligence with the ancient principles of acceptance, love, and compassion, principles we have known but have failed to live by regarding those whose sexualities and gender identities lie outside established norms. We need to replace our fear, demonization, and rejection with acceptance, humanization, and love. In other words, rather than seeing LGBTQ individuals as fully human, we have tended to dehumanize them, to treat them as prodigal, as deliberately devious and disobedient, as somehow "other," whether in our families, our communities, or our congregations. Changing how we see and respond to them is essential work. It is the work to which Christ calls us in his twenty-first-century church to undertake. In one of his last teachings (Matthew 25), he asks us to see people who are gay, lesbian, bisexual, transgender, and any others we may think of as "least" or lost as if they were Christ himself. Clearly, we have not yet fulfilled this call to higher discipleship.

Given how deeply they implanted the desire for dancing in the spirits and bodies of their mortal children, one must assume that our Heavenly Parents love dancing and find at least as much joy in it as we do. Tessa Morrison states that, "The bliss of heaven has been characterized by the dance of all the angels and the illumination of light." She also states that "Clement of Alexandria claimed that with the revelation of the Christian mysteries the initiated shall dance with the angels."[1] In the apocryphal gospel, "The Acts of John," Jesus's beloved disciple recounts that the night before his arrest and crucifixion, Jesus invited his apostles to circle him in a dance as he sang a hymn to them. From such ancient texts has derived the tradition of Jesus as "The Lord of the Dance."

In my imagination, I see a scene in which Jesus, the Lord of the Dance, leads us all—gay, straight, transgender, lesbian, bisexual, whatever our sexual orientation or gender identity—along with his angels in a dance of celebration "in the illumination of light."

---

1. From the abstract of "The Dance of the Angels, the Mysteries of Pseudo-Dionysius and the Architecture of Gothic Cathedrals," Analecta Husserliana: The Yearbook of Phenomenological Research 81, "Metamorphosis" issue (2004): 299–320.

SECTION 1

JOY IS COMPLICATED

TO DANCE IN THE DIM LIGHT: MEDITATION ON JOY, PART 1

KERRY SPENCER PRAY

I don't know that I thought much about joy growing up.

Once, when I was about seven, I remember riding my bike in a circle for an hour. It went from day, to twilight, to near dark. There was a cool wind as the sun went down. I rode and rode in the dim light. My brother called from where he had climbed far up in our pine tree. He always went much higher than I would dare; the top of the tree would bend with his weight, as he dangled from 30 feet up.

"What are you doing?" he yelled down at me.

I didn't answer. I was riding.

I looped the driveway once, twice, three times. It felt good to push against the pedals, good to push against my breath, to feel the pull of the centrifugal motion. *This is what it means to be alive,* I thought, as I circled and circled. *This feeling. This wind. This light. This motion.*

In church I sat in the cold folding chairs, the metal getting sweaty underneath my thighs. "What do you think it means to have joy?" my primary teacher asked me.

I kicked my feet up and down, looked at my shoes. I thought of how it felt to ride my bike at dusk, just motion and wind, and breath, and intent. *It feels like that,* I thought.

My teacher said things about obedience. Keeping the commandments. Making the right choices. Repenting.

It didn't sound like riding my bike. And so I didn't answer her question out loud.

If joy was something different than the feeling I had that night, I wasn't particularly interested in it.

In seminary we learned our scripture mastery. 2 Nephi 2:25. "Men are that they might have joy." I sat in the back of the seminary classroom. Class started at 5:15 a.m. I never wore makeup in high school (except to Mormon dances). Wearing makeup would have meant that I would have to get up earlier than 4:45 a.m. if I wanted to make it to the church building without getting a tardy. You couldn't go to BYU if you had too many seminary tardies, and BYU was the only school I was interested in.

The teacher said more things about obedience.

I was wearing my PE clothes, ready for my 6:00 a.m. gym class, and noticed a spot on my legs I'd missed when shaving. I pulled a razor out of my bag and held it in my hand so it was mostly hidden. My legs were so dry that when I ran the razor across them, white flecks of skin burst out in little clouds. I got the lotion out of my bag next.

"I can't believe you are shaving your legs in seminary, Kerry," my friend whispered to me. She was laughing.

I shrugged.

This lesson was boring. They kept saying "men are that they might have joy" as if that was supposed to mean anything to me, a fifteen-year-old girl. I knew what it was supposed to be, what they wanted me to say, what all the "right" answers, the "seminary" answers, were. Mormons talk in subtext. They might say, "men are that they might have joy," but what that *meant* was I, a girl, had to obey. I had to make the right choices. Go to the temple. Marry some boy there. Have a ton of babies.

Fine, well, that wasn't something I was doing right then. Right then I was thinking about the way the lotion stung my freshly shaved legs. Dry shaving was a bad idea, probably, but what else was I supposed to do, sitting in the back row of seminary with a giant patch of missed hair on my legs?

"Hey," said my friend. "Lend me that razor real quick."

I handed it to her.

"Are you SHAVING?" The seminary teacher stopped the lesson to scold us both.

I shrugged. My legs were hairy and I had a razor. It was five in the morning and seminary was boring. What was so weird about any of this?

He shook his head and turned back to the board. "I can't believe you are shaving in seminary," he said.

Joy is a complicated emotion.

I think we are all bothered by its complications. We think it should be simple. We think that it is happiness and laughter and moments that are unburdened by fetters and heartbreak and despair. And sometimes it is that. But when Mormons talk of joy, it's always linked to fetters: the law, obedience, making the right choices. If we do these things (we list them, on the board, like a to-do list) then we will have joy.

But joy is not simple.

And no list, no matter how comprehensive, or how strenuously adhered to, can make it simple.

———————

When I was a little girl, I started to see a woman when I prayed.

My eyes were always closed when I saw her, though I wasn't always kneeling. Sometimes I lay on my back, rigid, corpse-like. Sometimes I lay on my side, fetal and full of yearning.

My room smelled like humidity and wood the first time I saw her. I remember the frame of my waterbed, covered in my baby sister's teeth marks. I remember reaching for it, to feel the rough grooves. I remember rocking there in the bed. The water was gentle. Like a cradle.

I had been praying. (I often prayed, especially as a little girl.) I didn't mean to make her appear. I was falling asleep, probably. I was seeing the dream images that flash in front of your eyes right before you lose consciousness. It certainly never occurred to me she could be a god. God to me was Father God. He was kind, attentive, but irrevocably and ontologically male.

When I prayed, I spoke to Father God in formal tones, never wavering from the form of prayer taught to me in my primary classes.

Invocation.

Gratitude.

Petition.

Closing.

Sometimes, when I was full of that aching I never understood—sometimes I called him just Father. Sometimes I said "you," instead of "thee" or "thou." But when I prayed, right before bedtime, when I was falling asleep and reaching out with the primordial ache of wanting the divine, it was always a woman who appeared.

She kept appearing, even though I never asked her to. I don't know if she would have appeared if I'd asked.

She was a shadow.

A shape I saw on the back of my right—always my right—eye.

She was veiled, her face had no features.

But she was a woman.

I didn't know if she was the Virgin Mary, or maybe an angel. She couldn't be the Holy Ghost, he was a man (even formless) wasn't he? Maybe she was a memory of someone I knew? Someone from another time? Another place?

I didn't know who she was.

I only know she made me feel peace.

————————

I talked to my partner about this essay.

"When they asked me to put together a book of writing by queer Mormons, I asked them if I could put together a book about joy." I fumbled with the seam of my skirt, which was fraying. "I couldn't handle putting together another book that told the *whole* truth about what it means to be a queer Mormon. Because the whole truth is gut-wrenching. Knowing the whole truth is too much, even for me, who lived it. It's all so heavy."

"The problem," they said, "is joy is actually a really heavy emotion." They were scrolling Twitter, as they sometimes do when I'm talking to them. Sometimes it bothers me when they do this. Sometimes it doesn't. My fingers are always anxious too, always need to be moving. Sometimes it's easier to talk about hard things when you're looking away, not letting yourself get too close to them.

I looked over at my bookshelves, heavy with books. Joy was heavier than all of them.

"Happiness would be one thing," I said. "But I'm not talking about happiness, I'm talking about *joy*. Joy isn't joy unless it's … earned. It's defiant. It comes *after* pain. *After* struggle. It's the feeling of finally finding freedom when you have only ever been imprisoned."

They scratched their arms, like they do when they are thinking. "Maybe if you include some light moments, things that are joyful and full of laughter, but *feel* lighter. Maybe then it won't be as bad," they suggested. "You should add in that chocolate sauce story."

"The chocolate sauce SEX story?" I laughed.

"It is a *very* funny story," they said.

"You aren't wrong," I said. "But I was raised Mormon. Telling that story feels wild and risky."

"There isn't even any actual sex in that story, Kerry, what the heck."

I shrugged and laughed because there was not.

"Sex is one place there's joy," they said. "Even Mormons know that."

"True," I said. "But Mormons also have such a hard time thinking of queerness as being about anything *other* than sex. They get fixated on it and won't listen to the rest of what we say because we are deviant and you shouldn't let deviants poison your mind."

"I mean, deep down, they know. They know their marriages aren't just about sex. They know sex is one of many potential sources of joy. Not for everyone—not that they acknowledge asexuality as an option—but it is a place joy exists. Let the truth be the truth. Prudishness be damned."

"I will think about it," I promised them.

––––––––––––

When I was very pregnant with my first child, I desperately wanted a woman.

The wanting I felt was nothing I recognized as sexual. (Gayness was a simple sexual perversion, I'd been told. And I had no thoughts I could point to as perverted or even sexual.) I just ... I desperately needed a woman. To sit next to me. To be there when I gave birth. To hold my hand and laugh with me. To tell me things would be okay.

I was raised being told queerness was a choice. If I were to fall in love with a woman (which I had, rather dramatically, more than once) it was simply a temptation: one that would tempt anyone, really. What was important was that I not give in to the temptation. I was not *gay*, I was human. Satan tempts all humans to break the rules.

I dated men. I married the first one who didn't terrify me—a kind, sometimes feminine, man who looked at me with softness in his eyes. I wasn't much older than my son is now. It honestly didn't occur to me either one of us could be gay. (We both were.)

And then I was pregnant and desperately wanted a woman.

I didn't know what to make of it—the desperation.

It was unformed. Primal. Overpowering.

I told myself it was something biological, something to do with childbirth. Having a woman around would increase survival in my female ancestors. Which would explain it, I told myself. It would explain this confusing, overwhelming, need.

I remember pacing, giant belly too big in my tiny bathroom.

I was barefoot, the linoleum smooth against the soles of my feet.

I was too hot, too cold.

I washed my hands once, twice.

I pumped the soap, deliberately.

I washed every finger and then I reached out to dry them on a towel hanging on the wall. The friction of the towel was grounding, the rough feel of the terrycloth underneath my fingertips felt like reminding myself to breathe.

I could see the woman of my childhood prayers then—or rather an echo of her.

I cried out in the bathroom, holding my too-full belly in my hands. I was dizzy with it. The inexplicable *yearning*.

I must have put on shoes. I must have gotten a coat.

It was February and everything was frozen.

All I knew was that ... I ... needed.

I didn't know what.

I didn't know who to call or how to get it.

I didn't know how to pray to a Father God, not about this.

(Father God could never understand this kind of ache.)

It was dark as I drove.

I drove away.

My cell phone lost its signal as the lights of the city disappeared. I was deep in the desert.

I parked the car next to a pile of rocks at the bottom of a mountain of rocks. I sat on top of one of them, looking out at the starlight, watching the light reflect off the salt pools. The ground was all salt and dirt. Scatters of sage plants rustled anxiously in the wind. Almost nothing grew in the salt ground. The shadows of the mountains were long in the moonlight. They reflected in the saltwater pools. All I could see was shadow and mirror.

Barren.

It was barren.

It was such a relief, the barrenness. The salt and sand and moonlight and darkness rocked me, the way my childhood waterbed rocked me as I prayed myself to sleep.

Was I supposed to live with this incomprehensible aching? Why did it feel like something that would go away, if only a woman was there, in the dark desert sand, with me? Why did I feel like everything would be safer, if only she could take my hand? Why could I almost smell her perfume on the wind?

I wanted to stay until the aching let up, but I couldn't.

My contractions got harder and faster and I was alone and smart enough to panic. There would be no woman coming here, to the desert in the dark, two hours outside of my last cell phone signal.

So I drove myself home, giving no explanation to my husband when I got there.

———————

The church tells us not to poison our minds with things of Satan. Tells us to avoid "worldly" things. As if you can keep a child from being gay or trans by keeping them from knowing that queerness exists, that it is anything other than evil, deviant behavior. And in some ways it works: as a queer child, you grow up, you make the "right" choices, it doesn't occur to you you're queer because "queerness" is bad, isn't it? But what do you do when you have made all the "right" choices and that sadness, that yearning, that soul-deep aching never lets up? What do you do when all the efforts to keep you from knowing about queerness succeed and all you're left with is the inexplicable sorrow? The sense that the very divinity inside you is a sin?

———————

The day before Valentine's one year, I went to pick up a takeout order at the local bar. A woman sat there—a regular. She came in every day with her husband. He was seventy-two, he told me once, proudly. He had perfectly straight teeth (probably dentures, but I didn't ask) and a mustache that was slightly longer than his face. He drove a Hummer, which feels like an important detail. His wife was younger, maybe sixty. Her long hair was over her shoulder. She was halfway through a glass of Pinot Grigio, her cheeks pink.

I had written an essay about my Aunt Ortensia's half-drunk pink cheek's once. My Swedish (probably autistic) uncle, who had been single his entire life, eloped in his seventies with Ortensia, who was younger, maybe sixty. Every year, he would hire a mariachi band for her birthday. She would invite us over and he would serve us bread and she would drink wine and would dance and dance. She put her arms around me and spun me around the room. I had never danced with a drunk woman before. I was barely twenty, and had never had a cup of coffee, never had sex, never said the word "fuck," even in my mind. I was too afraid of rigid rules and would not break them, would not risk offending Father God. Joy was obedience, wasn't it? But that didn't matter to Ortensia. She spun me in circles on her patio as the mariachi band played. *I didn't know you could laugh like that,* I wrote, *dancing with a drunk woman.*

Someone else in my family read the essay and they tore it up in front of me. "How dare you," they said. "How dare you say such terrible things about someone who has only ever been good to you."

I was confused because I hadn't realized I'd said anything terrible at all. I'd written about her laughter. I'd written about how I had leaned outside of the rules, how she had helped me, and how when I got outside them, I didn't find despair or wickedness, I found *joy.*

"Don't ever show this essay to anyone," they said. "Ever again."

And so I did not.

The woman in the bar, with her Pinot Grigio and pink cheeks, did not look like my Aunt Ortensia. Ortensia was round and dark, with black curls that went to her shoulders. The woman at the bar had much longer hair, and she wasn't at all dark. But there was a delighted conspiracy in the way she motioned to me, smiling against her flushed cheeks.

"Where is your lady?" she asked me, meaning my wife.

"Oh," I said. "She's doing another errand. I'm just getting takeout."

She looked to the left and to the right. "It's Valentine's Day tomorrow. Are you ready? Because I am going to tell you what you need to do."

I was not at all ready—my wife did not particularly like Valentine's, which she called "VD Day," and we didn't really celebrate it—but I leaned in to listen.

"I have a plan," she said. "But first things first. How big is your bed?"

The scarf around her neck sparkled.

"Oh goodness," I said, because I didn't know how to answer her question. I only knew how to laugh.

"Is it big enough?"

I was not sure what to say.

Everyone nearby had turned to watch us talk.

"You're gonna need to get something," she said.

She motioned that I had to come closer, that she needed to whisper to me.

I had no idea what she was going to say.

"The most important thing," she said, "is that it is waterproof."

I started to laugh so hard that I couldn't stop. I bent over, laughing. Everyone around us watched me, as I could not find a way to form words. My laugh is loud when I have *not* lost it, and it was even louder now that I had.

"The waterproof mattress is important," she continued, oblivious to my laughing. "But the next part is even more important. You're going to need to obtain chocolate sauce."

My laugh went silent as it transformed into a wheeze. I could not make a single sound come out of me, except for a high-pitched whine of lost breath.

"This is where the artistry comes in," she said.

She took me by the elbow, like a conspirator. "The most important thing is the *smear*."

I started to nod. Like, yes, honey. Preach it. The most important thing is the *smear*.

"Once you have a good smear," she said, "comes the jumping."

"The JUMPING." I repeated.

She turned back to her wine glass and emptied it. Without looking at me she said, "That's our plan at least."

When I, again, lost control of my laugh and it had become something of a cackle, she winked at me, which only made me laugh harder.

Her husband held up his wine glass. Looked at me. Said nothing. Just nodded and drank.

It wasn't anything like obedience. But it was something like joy.

GOODNIGHT, BABY LION

JACLYN FOSTER

There's a trend on my corner of queer TikTok right now that makes me cry every time. The user speaks to their past self, telling them about their life, their relationships, their identity. Their teenage self is dismayed—caught up in the throes of shame and repression, working so hard to *avoid* becoming that person they'd always been warned against. But their consternation is interrupted by a joyful noise: the user's childhood self, jumping up and down, openly celebrating. "We did it!" "I'm not crazy?" "I get to have a girlfriend?" And then I pause the video and my chest shakes. It's happening right now, just remembering them in the vaguest terms.

I don't remember being a queer child.

I remember queer *moments*, of course, retrospective signs and signifiers that gradually surfaced in the years after I came out. Staring at my best friend during social studies, transfixed by the wave of her hair and the curve of her arm. Bursting into inexplicable tears when my mom bought a tomboyish pair of shorts from Old Navy and insisting she return them. Flipping through the laminated hairstyle book at Supercuts, longing for short hair and somehow knowing, deep down, that I couldn't ask for it.

(I did send a message to my younger self about that last one, posting a selfie in the parking lot the first time I cut my hair short. "Dear eleven-year-old Jaclyn: Your face is not too round and your mom will not be mad. Love, twenty-eight-year-old Jaclyn.")

But my mom tells me that when I was twelve or thirteen, shortly after these memories, I confided that I sure had been noticing my friend's changing bodies, and I was concerned I might be gay or bisexual. "Maybe," she had responded, "Or maybe you're just noticing because it's different and there's something to notice." I remember more queer moments after that—stroking my friend's arm as she grew out an ill-fated attempt to shave her arm hair, a seemingly outsized reaction to a friend moving away, and yes, noticing low-cut shirts and locker-room flirtations I was sure I wasn't allowed to be a part of. But I don't remember the moment where I put words to it. I don't remember the connection, as it was happening: *I might be gay or bisexual.*

Years after I came out, I got diagnosed with ADHD—expected—and Sensory Processing Disorder—unexpected. I'd noticed some senses could be overstimulating and had difficulty following conversations when there was background chatter around me. But in addition to noticing too much, it's also possible to notice too little—and to not notice that you're not noticing. An unusual tolerance for cold, for instance, or not feeling the pain of a cavity until after the dentist tells you it's there. When the not noticing applies to emotions, it's called alexithymia: the inability to identify and describe your feelings.

For instance: coming home from school day after day, describing the day as "good," and being utterly perplexed when your parents seemed to expect more detail beyond that—what else was there to say? Occasionally, saying "good" and immediately bursting into tears, without being able to explain why. Feeling confused and frightened by these outbursts and managing them by shoving the emotions even further down, deeper and deeper, where I didn't know I was feeling them at all.

During my freshman year of college, Kya noticed that I wasn't noticing. "I know you feel sad I'm leaving on a mission," she insisted, "it's okay. It's okay to feel that." We sat on the couch in a common area and she slowly, gently, but insistently pried free what I'd wrapped up tight. I didn't know how to describe it then, but it felt odd to cry in a way that let things out, instead of in a way that clawed feelings back from escape. She revealed my feelings, walked me through them once, and then left for two years straight. I wasn't sure whether to be grateful or mad about it.

The next few years felt like slowly unclogging a drain. Whatever the feelings had been like going in, their long anaerobic simmer had left them fetid, gnarled, and distinctly baneful. My attempts at home emotional plumbing only seemed to flood the basement and back up the toilets. Feeling my feelings, I was sure, was only making everything worse—and maybe it was time to condemn the house altogether, burn it down and take my chances in the next life on spiritual insurance money or a spiritual arson charge.

Jaclyn struggles with missing her family and being away from them in another country, is the only part I remember from my therapist's accommodation letter. "That's not the problem at all," I thought, then suddenly remembering the hours I'd spent in therapy discussing that exact thing. I came out to myself, then came out to Kya, then came out to everyone. I didn't come out to my therapist.

I don't know whether the alexithymia or the internalized queerphobia is why I don't remember being a queer child. But judging by my repeated response to other people's past queer childhoods on TikTok, not knowing what I was feeling didn't stop me from feeling it.

I don't remember being a queer child.

I don't know if I have a queer child.

When Zoë was about three years old, she started declaring herself a "boyn" every time she donned her New York Yankees baseball cap my dad had bought her. As far as I could tell, a boyn was her word for someone who is not quite a boy, but not quite a girl. "When you're a boyn, do you need a different boyn name? Or still Zoë?" I asked.

"Still Zoë!" she exclaimed, obstinately riding her scooter through the living room.

"Okay, Boyn Zoë," I said.

"No! Just Zoë!" She was a boyn, off and on, for about six months, then stopped.

At one point, she got a hold of some scissors and cut her hair—weeks before my sister's wedding. "I wanted it SHORT," she insisted. I googled "child pixie cut" and showed her some examples on kids who looked like her. "Like this?" She nodded.

"I don't know how to cut hair like that, and we can't go to a hairdresser right now because of the big germ—but I can cut it as short as I can." I took over the scissors and wound up making her look like Téa Leoni in *Jurassic Park III*. By the point in the pandemic I felt comfortable taking her to a hair salon, she wanted to grow it out again.

She was firmly a girl by the time I got pregnant again. I went to MHA in Park City having done a public acknowledgement of my visible bump, but before the twenty-week anatomy scan. To my surprise, I found other moms asking my advice.

"I'm fine with my kid being gay, but they say they're polyamorous, and I don't know how to feel about that. I don't mind what they do by themselves, but I would feel weird to have multiple partners of theirs over at once." She squinted up at me from her table, the bright June sunlight incongruous against the cold mountaintop wind. My anti-sunburn straw hat flapped loudly, and I shivered.

"Well, imagine one of your older kids got a divorce, but it was really amicable. And then they remarried, and their new spouse and their old spouse became best friends. So sometimes they all did things as a family, because it's easier to have three parents wrangling the kids at Lagoon or because it's nice to have all three parents over for birthday dinner. If you hosted that birthday dinner, you wouldn't feel uncomfortable having multiple partners of your kid over at once—you'd be glad they had so many people to love them. Polyamory is like that, except nobody has to get divorced." As a terminally monogamous person myself, I worried over my answer, but it seemed to help.

The next mom had a question that hit closer to home. "What are you going to tell Zoë about the baby's sex?" Kya wasn't out as trans yet, but in a way that made the question all the more gratifying, to have trans inclusivity recognized without an obvious reminder.

"Well, there's a lot of different opinions on the best way to handle it, but what we ended up telling Zoë was that when the baby is born, it's too young to tell us if it's a boy, or a girl, or something else. So the doctors and the parents look at the baby's body and make their best guess. But not everyone's bodies show their gender, so when the baby gets older, it can tell us if we guessed wrong or right."

The conversation had dropped off there, the keynote speaker standing up at the podium. I remembered Zoë's response when we'd had that discussion. "You guessed right with me," she proclaimed. "I'm definitely a girl!"

"Yep," I responded, "And if you get even older and decide we guessed wrong, that's okay too. Mimi didn't realize Grandma and Granddad had guessed wrong until she was all the way a grownup!"

Zoë had rolled her eyes in the way only children can when their parents explain the painfully obvious. "Yeah, I know moooom."

A few weeks later, I went in for my sixteen-week checkup, and to my surprise, they did an ultrasound at that one too. "Oh, that's definitely a boy," my OB said. "Usually I don't like to tell parents until twenty weeks because it's a little ambiguous at this stage, but that's definitely a boy." I felt surprised and surprised by my surprise. "What are we going to do with a *boy*?" I wondered, feeling a little silly about the question. Lots of lesbian couples raised boys. But somehow, I'd assumed it would be all girls.

"He'll be the only boy in the family!" I exclaimed.

"Well, the only boy in the family so far. I was a boy when I was a baby," Kya joked.

I rolled my eyes.

"I mean, yeah, he's a boy, but he's also just a baby," she reassured me.

When he was born, I forgot to tell the doctors to towel him off first. They plopped him right on my chest, all wet and goopy in a way I'd been sure would be a sensory problem. His dark eyes bored into mine, and I stared back. Zoë had needed respiratory therapy right after birth, but he just looked around, all new senses in a brand-new world. The hospital was busy, and the nurses forgot about us for an hour, apologizing profusely when they returned. I wasn't mad. The whole time had had an overpowering sense of *rightness*—that he was meant to come here, that he was meant to be ours.

They were out of blue baby blankets. They wrapped him in pink, apologizing again, and we laughed and laughed after they left. We posted the picture on Instagram, and my grandma gave my dad money for a baby gift. "I don't care what you buy him, as long as it's blue!" she had exclaimed. "They're only dressing him in pink!"

I dressed him in anything, from any section. Stores had "gender neutral" sections that hadn't been as prominent or as full when Zoë was born, and I noticed some themes to their offerings. "Ah yes, the three baby genders: boy, girl, and a little bear," I joked. My baby was enormous, ninety-ninth percentile for height. I started to call him my little Levi Bear.

Zoë had struggled to feed as a baby, but Levi ate like a Roman senator, gorging himself until he vomited and then insisting loudly that his empty tummy be refilled. "Who's my hungry boy," I cooed, then immediately remembered another trending TikTok: "Imma fight these gender norms ... damn! These gender norms got hands!"

"Who's my little Totino," I corrected myself, my sleep-deprived brain remembering an SNL sketch where a beleaguered housewife making Sunday football snacks for her "hungry guys" gets unexpectedly pulled into a torrid sapphic art film with Kristen Stewart. "It's not like he knows what SNL is," I thought, "but then again, it's not like he knows what gender norms are either. Neither nickname is going to have any effect on him at this point."

Somehow while keeping a newborn baby alive, I was expected to teach Zoë to read. Kya had just come out as trans, and while Zoë had been well-adjusted to the idea when it was our private family dynamic, having the whole family respond to Kya as a woman at the same time as a new baby brother—when we had just moved apartments!—felt like too much change at once. I thought maybe we could kill two birds with one stone. I bought children's book after children's book about queer families, queer children, queer identities in general, and when they didn't answer everything I wanted them to, I wrote my own.

The idea came to me in a flash. In the rush to write it down, I couldn't have remembered where I kept my notebooks if my life depended on it. I seized the back of an old monthly calendar and one of Zoë's chewed-up rainbow pencils and frantically scrawled, "*Baby Lion and Daddy Lion lived together on the savannah. Baby Lion loved how Daddy Lion would race her to the far-away baobab tree, wrestle her in the tall grass, and cut her dinner into bite-sized pieces every evening...*"

My hand was cramping by the time I finished. Assured it was committed to paper, I sat back, massaging my right hand with my left. Feeling slightly foolish, I retrieved my laptop from my backpack and began to transfer it into a more legible format. "*... But most of all, she loved Daddy Lion's mane. It was soft, and fluffy, and smelled like the summer breeze—perfect for cuddling into at the end of a long day. Every night she would snuggle up in that mane and whisper, 'Good* *night, Daddy Lion. I love you.' And Daddy Lion would whisper back, 'Good night, Baby Lion. I love you too."*

I frowned. There was no way Zoë would sit through the whole story without pictures—but my stick figures were unlikely to capture her attention any better than the plain text. I began searching through stock photos of lions. Ctrl + C. Ctrl + P. The mundanity of doing battle with the image formatting contrasted oddly with the creative process. *No, wrap text, goddammit,* WRAP TEXT.

But one morning Baby Lion woke up to a strange sight. "Oh no!" she cried, "Somebody has stolen your mane while we were sleeping!"

Daddy Lion chuckled. "Nobody stole my mane," she said, "I shaved it off."

"Shaved it off? Why?" Baby Lion frowned.

Daddy Lion got a serious look on her face. "Well, it was a very good mane," she explained, "so soft, and fluffy, and perfect for snuggles. But I've always felt like a Mommy Lion on the inside. Every time I saw my reflection in the watering hole, it made me feel sad, because it didn't match who I wanted to be."

Fortunately, male lions gazing into watering holes seem to be a popular subject among wildlife photographers, but I wished I had the skills to Photoshop the reflection into a maneless lion. The metaphor felt hopelessly on the nose from an adult perspective, but I still wasn't sure Zoë would make the connection.

Well, I had done my best. "Zoë," I called, "come read this book with me."

She wrinkled her nose. "That's not a book, that's your computer!"

"It's a book I wrote on my computer. It's about a baby lion!" Zoë peered doubtfully at the screen, then cooed at the photos I had selected of the cub. For the moment, she snuggled into me.

Baby Lion thought for a minute. "But if you're my Mommy Lion, who will race me to the far-off baobab tree?"

"I will," Mommy Lion replied. "I don't need a mane to do that. Ready, set, go!" And off they ran.

"That tree looks weird!" Zoë said, "It's upside down!"

"They grow in Africa," I replied, "You saw one at the zoo with Granny and Grandpa, remember?"

Zoë looked doubtful. "Are they real?"

"Yes."

She cocked her head. "Is this book real?"

I paused. "Well it's a pretend book. But the baby lion is like you, and the Mommy Lion is like Mimi, where she used to be a Daddy. And the baby lion isn't sure if things are going to feel different now."

Baby Lion skidded to a stop and sat down to rest in the tree's shade. After a moment she asked, "But if you're my Mommy Lion, who will wrestle with me in the tall grass?"

"I will," Mommy Lion replied. "I don't need a mane to do that." And she rolled over and over with Baby Lion until she felt dizzy with giggles and her tummy started to rumble.

I tickled Zoë, and she squealed and rolled off the couch. I smiled, lifting her back into my lap to continue reading. "No, more tickles," she complained. I tickled her again, longer this time, until she was gasping for breath. She lay still, panting, and I seized my chance to continue reading.

"But if you're my Mommy Lion, who will cut my dinner into bite-sized pieces?" wondered Baby Lion.

"I will," Mommy Lion grinned, showing off her sharp teeth. "I don't need a mane to do that. And tonight we're having water buffalo—your favorite!"

"What's a water buffalo?" Zoë interrupted.

"You know, in *Lion King*. They have the big horns? They look kind of like cows?" I sighed. Zoë shook her head, so I pulled out my phone and looked up some pictures.

Zoë frowned. "Lions EAT THEM? For FOOD?"

"Yeah, lions are carnivores," I explained, "Like T-Rex. Listen to the story, okay? We're almost done."

Baby Lion chewed slowly while she thought. The sun was getting low in the sky, but she still had one last question. "But if you're my Mommy Lion," she yawned, "who will cuddle me when I go to sleep?"

"I will," Mommy Lion answered. "I don't need a mane to do that."

Baby Lion cuddled up to Mommy Lion. Her fur was short, and sleek, but it still smelled like a summer breeze. She snuggled in and whispered, "Good night, Mommy Lion. I love you." And Mommy Lion wrapped her paw around Baby Lion to pull her in close while she whispered back, "Good night, Baby Lion. I love you too."

I looked expectantly at Zoë. She stared at the computer screen, her brow slightly furrowed, and I tried to give her time to process, waiting for her reaction.

"Can I go watch Minecraft videos on the iPad now?"

"Sure," I sighed, "But you have to practice your sight words after dinner."

One day, we read *Pink Is for Boys*, a book with a simple message: colors don't have a gender and are fair game for everyone. We finished the last page, and she frowned. "But what about kids like Cassie?" Zoë asked, referring to a non-binary classmate of hers.

I was surprised. "That's a good question," I said slowly. "In some ways, books like this are helpful for people like Cassie. When there's so many silly rules that certain things are only for boys or only for girls, it's hard if you're not a boy or a girl, because it can feel like there isn't *anything* that's for you. But on the other hand, this book kept saying 'boy boy boy, girl girl girl,' but it didn't talk about people like Cassie at all. Are you worried that would make her feel left out?"

Zoë nodded.

"That's a good point," I said, "I'm glad you remembered it."

I don't know if I have a queer child. If I do, I don't know if either of them will remember *being* a queer child. But I know they'll remember being around queer people and having the words to discuss it. And whether it's theirs or mine, I know they'll remember the joy.

BLUE JAYS, I MEAN TOO JAY'S

DAVID DOYLE

I first met Kris online as they were first coming out and exploring what it means to not identify as the gender they grew up being told they were. They also posted selfies with their blue hair and bright blue eyes, and lots of pictures of screaming possums, which I thought was quite quirky.

We messaged each other quite a bit as we discussed some of the challenges and experiences we had as queer Mormons, wondered how we fit in God's plan, and that we wanted things to be better for the next generation of LDS queer people.

"I don't mind having an agender spirit but it'll be weird if I'm the only one :P"

"Hopefully you and I can help educate the cranky old dudes and teach them how to make things better and not worse :-)"

Kris, simply for being themself in this church and standing up for themself, wound up receiving national attention from the likes of the *Washington Post*, *The Advocate*, *ABC News*, and more. Kris made a point to be visible to show other trans kids there are people like them.

Thanks to the news coverage, many queer people got in touch and Kris tried to reply to everyone. I know that if Kris was aware of a queer person going through financial difficulties, Kris would often send some money.

Kris had family in Florida and when they came to the state for a visit, we made a point to get together. On one such visit, I picked up Kris and went to Too Jay's Deli, a popular eatery in Orlando. It was mid-morning on a weekday and we walked in to find we were the first customers to arrive for lunch.

In front of us was a tall, scrawny young man with purple hair, several earrings, colorfully painted fingernails, and a rainbow pin on his jacket. "Welcome to Blue Jays," he said, bungling the greeting as he nervously intertwined his fingers. "I mean TOO JAY's. I am so sorry. This is my first day working here. I'm so sorry. Welcome to Too Jay's."

It was obvious this greeter was queer. He didn't have to say anything, we could tell just from looking at him.

Kris smiled and asked, "Is this establishment a safe place for queer folks?" Just like that, all the awkwardness was gone.

The server's worried look disappeared as he displayed a smile. "I am queer! I am so glad you're here! Are you queer? Wait, I don't think I'm supposed to ask that. Sorry. Follow me, I'll show you to a table."

By asking if it was a safe place for queer people, Kris indicated this queer server was safe with us and his nervous walls came down.

"Why yes, we are queer. My friend David is gay and I'm trans. Thank you for noticing."

The server kept coming by much more than was necessary. As he took our orders and refilled our glasses, he started telling his life story.

"I only came out two years ago. My parents were upset. I didn't know what to do. I met a guy who let me crash at his place and we became boyfriends. Only, he was a jerk and I didn't realize it was a bad relationship. It was my first one, I had nothing to compare it to.

"I brought you more Diet Coke. My ex and I had lots of fights and I broke up with him. That meant I had to move out. I'd saved some money and decided to have a fresh start. Orlando seems neat so I moved here. I don't know anyone yet but I'm looking forward to meeting new people."

Kris kept reassuring him that he was doing fine. We could see his confidence grow. By the time we finished lunch, there was a bond between us, this server now felt like family.

Before we left the restaurant, Kris asked to see the manager and gave the server a glowing review.

We told a friend of ours who is nonbinary about our lunch experience and how adorable it was to watch this employee go from nervous Nelly to chatty Kathy as he was excited to talk with the first queer people he'd met since moving to Orlando. Our friend loved hearing our encounter and wanted to meet the server.

The three of us returned a few days later. As we walked in, the server recognized us and beamed a smile a mile wide.

"Heeeyyyyyy!!! I'm so glad you're back! When you were here before, that was my first day as a server, not just at Too Jay's, but ever. They hired me on a trial basis to see if I could hack it. When I found out you spoke to the manager and told him such nice things about me, I about cried. You don't even know what that meant to me."

It was wonderful to see Kris make an impact like this. I vowed to be more like them.

Later that year, my friend Kris passed away. I was unable to travel out of state to attend their memorial service. Instead, I invited some queer friends to come with me to Too Jay's. I relayed about coming to this deli with Kris and why I chose to have us all gather here. Those who knew Kris shared some of their memories. The mood was tender as we laughed at the things Kris did and their obsession with possums, commented on the huge impact Kris had in our queer LDS community, and lamented that Kris was gone.

I still think of Kris and the lessons they taught me, such as queer joy can be found in simple acts and to look out for each other. Kris also taught me to be authentic and open with others, to be optimistic while recognizing pain and disappointments, pursue your passions, and laughter always helps. The memory of Kris helps me generate queer joy in my life.

ANOTHER EXTENDED METAPHOR OF AN OCEAN VOYAGE, AS A PROSE POEM ABOUT QUEER JOY

ZV HAWKES, JOYFUL QUEER

The Sargasso Sea is almost invisible, a sea with no shores. It is a vast expanse of the Atlantic Ocean that is bounded by currents rather than land, a million-acre "eye" of the planet's largest whirlpool. The Sea, itself, barely moves. It's a creepily quiet place of stagnation and stillness, where the water spins in from the Caribbean Gulf Stream on the west, or the North Atlantic Current, or the Canary Current on the east, or the North Atlantic Equatorial Current sweeping up from Africa, and back west to the Caribbean. Once trapped in the Sargasso Sea, the water becomes much warmer than the currents' moving water, and forests of sargassum seaweed grow to hundreds of yards wide and long, while floating only a meter or so deep.

> (I was only a meter or so deep. You see that clearly as
> the sea sees)

The further in toward the middle you go, the clearer, and stiller, the water becomes. Deeper and deeper blue, and almost black. You would expect it to be green, but it is more frightening than that. Sediment brought from shores loses all momentum and sinks, and islands of sargassum appear, harboring small native creatures and transient migrating species that feed on the mix of weed and smaller prey animals. The one piece of land visible from inside the sea is visible from its western-most boundary: Bermuda.

> For all its reputation as the place where ships disappear,
> the Bermuda Triangle is the scary folkloristic answer to the
> deceptively ravenous Sea. Samuel Taylor Coleridge's "Tale

of the Ancient Mariner" features the Narrator's experience becalmed in the Sargasso Sea, including the famous lines "Water, water everywhere, and all the boards did shrink;/ Water, water everywhere, nor any drop to drink." There is a long history of ships lost to the Sargasso Sea, since once inside, there may not be provisions enough for the man-power to move a ship back into the currents it strayed from, and disoriented, dehydrated sailors can perish before they recognize the danger.

Here, though, the Sargasso Sea is my life before I became un-stuck, Life in the Before Times. Like a little Sargasso Sea creature of some kind, I was born there. It is all I knew, my old delusions, its seeming safety and stillness. Its warmth; my security and blissful ignorance of Before-Times choices: the hetero marriage I was in, my old job, my Mormon religion assuring me that the still, quiet, warm, placid and obedient Safety it gave me was preferable to everything else. A Meter or so deep. But easy in its simplicity: there's *a* right and *a* wrong to *every* question there; one of two choices is always (not always, not hardly ever) preferable to more choices; to motion, or change, or variegation, or learning, or breathing, or recognizing quiet desperation, or becoming real.

As I grew there, chose to stay there the way an eight-year-old child "chooses" to be baptized, I once or twice had exposure to something else, but I pushed it away. From these motion-less clear but black waters, once or twice, the thought of an island in a cooler sea, a steep-floored beach overbuilt with lava or rocks, or even a slow-growing, windswept coldwa-ter coral, once—or twice—intruded into my inexperience. Those rare times I was keeping myself safe, I thought, or I dreamed, of a breathtaking thing—place? that I thought I knew I wanted, knew I needed to reach, without knowing (or "daring speak") its name or coordinates or how to get there, or if I ever would reach it.

The thing wasn't necessarily Paradise. It was still, somehow, life; life is always life-full, but what pulled on me, hidden and tempting, was as different from the Sargasso Sea as a sea slug is different from a pinecone, or a Tuesday, or an adverb. From far off, as I bobbed gently on the sargasso weeds, this different thing, a way to be that was—in motion, in action—? It was the difference between freedom and fear. That distant thing felt like freedom. The dream felt as real as a dream feels, and idyllic, distant, too exotic to be safe.

If I ever thought, in my waking life, that I encountered it—shades of it, whatever it was, I doubled down on the safety of safety. I once discovered that a celebrity I had hardly ever noticed had been killed in an accident, and it struck me harder than some deaths of relatives had. I grieved hard for days, and I had never had any interest in following celebrities in general or this one in particular. The grief was double: it hurt, but it baffled.

The fear got worse.

Married too young, I always harbored the grim and damning knowledge that something was wrong with me. I was broken. My heart did not work as it should.

The prophets all promised: two good people, obedient, chaste, Good People, would not *be* incompatible. If they live the Gospel, all the important parts were covered. It was a prophetic blessing and a promise.

And I tried. I was so good at trying. And still I found: I was cold and unloving at the deep-down core of myself. One time, just once, (out in *public*), with my husband, both of us near middle-aged, I watched a young couple in love, ecstatically happy, laughing, staring hungrily at each other, touching hands, eager— Two fears reared at me together: one, that my husband should see me looking at them; that anyone should notice me notice them. And two, that as my whole chest-ribcage-shoulders-stomach heaved to join them and all of my body to follow, running away and running toward, *that is* WRONG! hissed at me with all the strength of the whispery sargasso winds. (I must, must join them.) (I *absolutely* must, must *not* join them!)

They were both girls.

It was the shock for me, at the time.

Never said it would shock you reading this in here.

I bit my tears back, frightened, confused, and angry with shame, and returned to the Sargasso Sea for many, many more years.

> Then from about 2016 to at least 2021 my life, like yours, and yours, and yours, and yours, and all of yours, was thrown into chaos. My own individually-tailored, me-shaped chaos was the pull of currents—out of the sea, into the Ocean.

Currents became ir-resist-ableandIwasPulled, pulledwithoutmywillinsidemywillshocky and blinking from my Sargasso Sea, into the swift-gasp-cold current of the ocean,

by a love at once both waiting (half lifetimes), and raw-new vulnerable and brutal and uniquely impossible:

I had to contend with reality

Outside the Sea, a new reality of not-the-sea.

of the Island-thing-place-notquiteParadise.

Which was no longer distant.

I found myself face to face with the rest of the Ocean, well beyond the Sargasso; a trembling new person made of nerve endings from inside of myself, a whole new adolescence: I was/am/always have been *not* intimately cold, but contained; in fear of myself: a lesbian in a hetero-insistent world. But I was not incapable of love, I could love.

> I could LOVE. But wrongly-love, shunned-love, un-love. Counterfeit—

> > Counterfeit love. Not love.

I loved

Whether I wanted to or

Not.

And it was still Love. Or rather, it was, Here, Middle-aged Person: meet Love. All my other late-blooming, late-to-come-out friends have said of their own release, and I said it of mine, more than once, "So this is what the poets were talking about. So *this* is what the music and the plays and the art and the wars fought and.

"Oh.

"*This*.

"Of course."

It was Joy, I had been hiding from, afraid of, heeding the words of the prophets about—the gold-colored rule they followed to do to me what *they* wanted, what brought joy to *them*, was not designed to bring joy to me. Even though they believed it, and I believed it (as hard as I could with all my might and main) Joy was what I had feared so valiantly, so stridently. Joy, and freedom, and Love.

In the Before Times, when faced with straight, heteronormative, witness-comfortable, old-person-smile-inducing, Correct, Social-ly-Not-Squicky love (and I *faced* it—I wanted to want it, I yearned for it, I knew I *needed* it, I knew it was the thing that made anything worth doing, life worth living—),

> I was cold (and *paralyzed* with heartbreak) because I *could* not constitutionally;

> but,

> faced with gay love, queer love, "bad" love, "wrong" love, the love that so Famously Dared NOT Speak Its Name

> I was cold because I w/could not, conceptually.
> *I* was Mormon, and *that* was sin.
>> And I had run away faster than I recognized what from.

Yet now, in my fifties and in love for the first time "properly" (as in, fully aware of and acknowledging my sexuality, her sexuality, and the havoc—however carefully I moved, in whatever direction—I was about to set loose on my little world, determined to pursue a relationship which I stubbornly *did* not see was doomed from every angle), I understood immediately (1) how strange it was, to be a sea creature, and yet live only in the Sargasso Sea.

(2) how pathetically, sub-microscopically tiny and useless and sad the accusation is, that (my) nature is unnatural. That they could think of Love and Sin as so close

Nature is big.

Bigger than two.

Nature is bigger than me and bigger than the planet,
> which has the water,
>> which swirls among land masses,

which produce streams of currents—one vortex in
particular—
    which produces a Sea,
        which grows constantly with weeds,
            which float on warm clear, deadly water.
Nature is bigger than the biggest star and galaxy; Nature has
universes.

NATURE has upwards of eighteen configurations of species-wide
and species-specific sexual, asexual, and demisexual ways of propa-
gating critters—that science has *counted so far*. Including hundreds
of genetic, epigenetic, chemical, *in oocyte, in blastocyst, in utero, ex
utero* conditions and permutations and vulnerabilities that can and
might and may and could and would and sometimes do arrange, all
alone or in any number of admixtures and combinations and degrees
and gradations *just* the *biological* morpheme of an individual organ-
ism of the species *Homo Sapiens*, which can influence sexuality in
that individual.

Jesus! What a discovery to make half a century into this
mess: Mormon God is corporeal, and the size of Jesus. But if
Love feels like this, then God is going to have to grow up, or
something. And if God is bigger than Nature, I think God can
handle all the things we find so weird and frightening, and God
can look at us trembling in fear and rage and accusation of the
icky and smile indulgently and say—again—just Love One Another. That is All.

Another thought to pair it: How tiny, tiny, minis-
cule is a god that works by codes of sin, and its tiny,
itty-bitty companion, righteousness. Tiny little god,
try to be so scary. We stomp it now.

(What an exotic, special little hell the Churches set us all up for, all
those millennia, centuries, greed and terror tricking them into theft
from Nature: old frightened Men, commandeering and appropri-
ating the functions of wonder and love and romance and appetite,
mystery and ecstasy and sexual expression—joy, pleasure, connection, transcendence, ineffability—claimed and locked up, their

permission gingerly distributed and reclaimed; the rights of such distribution belonging only to those with Authority to own it all; to own the Nature which produced them, or the God who did (arrogance doesn't quibble except about words). Over the years of this world: a million tiny churches or One Grandly tiny Church, lying

> its rank breath through thin sour lips and yellow teeth that their Plan has more happiness for all to receive than *loving* and *being* loved!

This whirlwind
—flight
from sargasso weeds to land, solid reality, a continent? an Island? was entirely new, beautiful, outrageous. And disorienting and terrible because it put me through New Puberty during Actual Menopause. Before I'd even caught my breath of First True Love, it launched right into First True Breakup. A stodgy, Jell-O-eating, sensible-shoes-wearing teacher, I was spun, like a Disney dragon-hag, into the crazy ex-girlfriend I had never been when I was straight.

"When" I was straight, my heart had never been broken like that. It had never been opened like that. *Inhabited* like that. (Like I had inhabited hers?)
Shattered and pulverized like that.

A queer friend—a *marriage counselor*—told me, "There's break-up crazy, and then there's broke-up *Lesbian* crazy, and Girl? Nothing comes even close."
Yes. He was correct. I'd had no practice or warning that this could happen to me. I was pushing sixty chronologically, supposed to be a grown-up—I looked like a grownup. but I was emotionally fifteen, *thirteen*, sobbing my melodramatic confusion and pain-rage in a dank and badly lit gym locker room, watching cliques of real-life and social media friends flock away from me and toward the pretty girl I could not have, whom I had introduced so many of them to, flock to her in their abject sympathy for *her* as she shared her plight, their sorrow for what she was going through, adoring her and cheering her on through Pride Month and Beyond, as she grew
> away from me and into a new thing,

… as I was a new thing
And me, doing all the watching and raging and weeping, and
watching a
  family or
        two,
        dis integrate,

        (because they told me, they promised me, us, all of us,
        that no two obedient Members—)
        dis-integrated.
all from inside that lonely-ass closet. With everything I ever knew
and built recoiling from me and my chaos as it all crumbled. I was
my membership in that church. It was my personality. (Well, it was
a chunk of persona.) Crouched in the closet with the shoes and the
old fusty coats and the dust of old ideas and the old living-room ele-
phants and their skeletons, I didn't know what was outside the door
(Well, I knew *who* was—had been—wasn't anymore—not my *reason*
for burning it all down, but the trigger for it; the match.)

I came out to my family accidentally. The turning point to reality
happened in such a state of dreams, but my new understanding of
the "identity" I had always run from—that unfurled as "by itself" as
it could have done.

  And suddenly my husband knew. He read a letter I had
  sub-conscientiously left open on the family computer, and he
  knew. Married decades, with a sweet and shame-scorched "eternal" companionship I could never force all the way to the Love I
  had found—not there—

    By that time I was out of the Sargassum, well into the
    breakers, the close-up, slam-you-into-the-coral churning,
    the disorienting wave-crash where the force of a million
    tons of seawater curling into itself tugs the surfboard's an-
    kle-leash clear off your leg and threatens to dislocate a knee
    while it does; you can drown inhaling the deceptively airy
    softness of foam; you can be broken if you think you know
    where "up" is; you can lose everything if you swim, you will
    die if you fight.

The only way to survive is counterintuitive: relax, go limp, let the water have its way. You can't fight the ocean. Really, honestly. The ocean is the truth about yourself—myself.

And: this is interesting: The Ocean has never been anything to fight. This was a truism long before the renowned King Canute showed one way or the other.

As you all know, the joy comes in the quitting.

To quit: to stop.

To quit: to leave.

So when I quit the Sargasso Sea, I struggled; when I quit my struggle, there was joy. Here is the answer to the question that plagued me so often in the Sargasso Sea. The Q: Is this feeling in my stomach, my solar plexus, that trembles—is it the Devil tempting me *toward* evil, or is it the Holy Ghost, warning me *away* from the evil? Here is the A: Though the choice feels like fear, one response feels like submission, and the other response feels like FREEDOM. Seek the freedom. And surrender, but do not submit.

Only limp as a rag tossed and moved and shaped, in the release the unclench the motion and action, and wave-curl and smash. But the battering will change in surrender: finally able to trust that the ocean was bigger than me, so I could not impose anything on it; the ocean was also bigger than the surf around my little Reality Island, and, it was bigger than the Sargasso Sea ever was and ever had been.

I released more and more old assumptions and expectations. Including the expectation that I would—or could—make it to shore unchanged or make it to shore at all. I released the assumption that the sea and the surf and the waves were an enemy. Indifferent, yes. But indifferent means "not cruel" as much as it means "not kind."

Surrendering—releasing the past, letting go of the Before Times— was not as hard for me or for my sake as I thought it would be; giving up the life I had lived for over half a century, that's what hurt most, by far, not mine but the pain which struck so many whom I loved.

So there were times I did fight, and though it was the hard way, and stupid, and it did break things, at least I kept all my beloved people.

Almost all.

Those I lost, I lost (by) fighting, straining; (by) clinging. In the pounding surf, effort makes brittle; flailing kills, while the flexibility of a submitted, trusting body or mind or soul matches the inevitable swirl and bend of the current, and in matching it, the body, or the soul, gains if not the power of the sea, at least the shape of this tiny bit of it, and the foam re-softens into foam, instead of deception.

It's many-layered. Because even during the tumult of change, I knew it would end; I knew how and why certain (not all) parts of it would end, I knew *when* it would end. I visited a dear friend, the first person I came out to

> (who told me it was FABULOUS news and that several of our mutual acquaintances had been 'shipping us getting together for maybe *years*: I am so old I had to be filled in on what "shipping" meant, in such a context),

and I said, "I am going to love her. It will burn my old life down, and it will make my life an absolute wreck for … three to five years.

"Bring. It. ON!"

And then Dear Friend and I both cackled and cackled at the hilarity of how desperately horrible I was about to make my life.

> (—and at the weird sharp sting of bliss shooting too fast from the little unhatched thing I was just barely cracking open, brand new in my life; death to so much I had built—I knew it was a terrible, terrible idea, and I wanted it, *and* I could imagine the ending.)

It would take three to five years. My marriage would end; he and I would still be friends and his journey would be his own and he is happy with a kind and lovely *straight* wife who adores him as I could not. I would probably lose my first love (but I really hoped not); I did.

I would have a chance for love and connection with others, maybe, probably. But it would be in the second or third year, if I could relinquish my hold on delusions, I would find and love the person most suited to me, best for me of all I could ever want.

This too happened. She came from her own end of the Sargasso Sea, through pain and loss and grief and wonder and hope (and

Mormonism). I love and I am loved: we Love like poets (but less dysfunctional), in the tumult of the truth about myself and herself and ourselves, and the truth about the two of us. The children—mine and my ex-husband's; hers and her ex-husband's—grow and grow and keep being who they are, which now is no longer children. I would soon leave my hometown and my children's; they would as well. They are on their own and they visit us often.

And the happily ever after would be—is—each moment of awareness, each breath, every sip of cool water or bite of good food, every glimpse of sky or cloud. And every empty-nest pang and every deep doubting night of reflection on the pools of regret we drank so deeply from, for so many years. We learn and learn; we hurt and stumble and hurt and laugh; now, let's dance.

I knew it would happen like this. This was always on its way. Fear, my hated, hated companion, assured me of this, *because* I was afraid of this very bliss, and did not know it. Even in that terrified beginning, and even in the desperately sad stretches, some so long, I knew oncoming joy was as inevitable and irrepressible as the force of the crashing waves and the tug of the moon on the tides. I knew with absolute clarity of purpose where, in the chaos, I was heading:

I would be a while in the waves,
and a while staggering dizzily through the little tidepools farther in.
And another while walking through knee- and ankle-deep water,
until I felt the kindness of fine clear sand
under my feet.

But well before then, as I fumbled, gracelessly submitted in the agitation of surf, there were glorious moments when the ocean itself, in an indifferent, coincident surge, lifted my face to the surface and into the sun-yellow air, gasping, but laughing, not only not dead, but not afraid, and more alive than before; more alive and more alive and *more* alive, body and soul mingling with the salt sand crash and chaos of joy.

TAKE MY WHOLE LIFE TOO:
A GAY MORMON SAYS GOODBYE
TO HIS MOM

TROY WILLIAMS

I'm standing with my family on a rain-soaked jetty on the Oregon Coast in the winter of 2009. My numb fingers grasp a cardboard box holding my mother's remains. The ocean crashes violently against the rocks but I try to keep myself and her ashes dry from the storm. We are a typical American family: me the gay activist, my sister the Tea Party enthusiast, and my father, the devout Latter-day Saint. Plus we have an Elvis impersonator from Orem. None of these things seem quite like the other, which is how my family has always been. Yet we huddle together at odd angles on a sodden gray December afternoon to say our final goodbye.

How did Elvis arrive at mom's funeral in Eugene? Well, she was a super fan. Most Latter-day Saints adorn their homes with portraits of Joseph Smith and Jesus. Oh no, not mine. Mom's extensive collection of Elvis LPs, VHS tapes, porcelain statues, and other King-inspired kitsch might not have impressed more ardent fans, but it certainly attracted attention from our houseguests. As a teen, I was mortified by Mom's memorabilia. In her sewing room, she had even hung a large framed picture of young hot Elvis, on genuine black velvet.

I thought it unrefined, perhaps even idolatrous. I was ashamed. And yet, Elvis brought her joy.

As Mom's breast cancer progressed beyond treatment, she began to plan her funeral—or, as she wanted it called, her Celebration of Life. She wasn't going to leave something so important in the hands of my father. And she was also adamant that the service be held in the senior center they liked to attend—not the local ward house. Initially I thought this was because she wanted me and my sister who were not active in the church to feel welcome. I thought this was all very sweet, until I discovered the deeper truth.

Mom told us that her final wish was to have her favorite Elvis impersonator from Utah perform at her celebration—and she knew that would never fly with her bishop! There would be no traditional church service with organ music and pious sermons about the atonement of Christ. Mom wanted a concert.

I was proud of her for being unorthodox, and also relieved. Just one year earlier, we learned that the church had funneled millions into California's Proposition 8, to restrict the freedom for people like me to marry who we loved. It had only been a couple years prior, and tensions between LGBTQ and LDS folks were still at an all-time high. I dreaded walking back into the cinder-block halls of my parents' ward.

At the time, I produced a progressive talk show on a Salt Lake radio station, KRCL. The *Salt Lake Tribune* had recently dubbed me "the gay mayor of Salt Lake City," an honorary position I, admittedly, was never actually elected to. But I did have a particular passion to make Utah as absolutely gay as possible (by 2017, Gallup would rank Salt Lake City as "the 7th gayest city in America" per capita—and I like to think something I did helped our ranking).

I was known back in the day for being a rabble-rouser activist, leading protests and kiss-ins around the Salt Lake Temple, and being hauled away in handcuffs while protesting at the Utah Capitol. Occasionally, to my father's horror, the Associated Press would run a story about gay activists in Utah, and my picture would end up in the Eugene Register Guard—fist in the air.

People in the ward knew I was a troublemaker, and it was a terrible embarrassment for Dad. My mom also remained quiet about it all, but blame shifted regularly. "Your father doesn't like us to discuss these things," she would say.

Mom died in early December, and we had decided to throw her party on the 28th—which would have been their fiftieth wedding anniversary.

I fly into Eugene two days before the service. My sister, Tammy, is on edge with preparations. She shouldered the burden of caring for my mother during her final months, dealing stoically with a dying body in ways Dad couldn't. I should have shown up more to help; I feel guilty that I didn't. The last time I saw my mom was Thanksgiving. We hadn't been particularly close over the previous ten years. When I came out, my parents' religious views on "same-sex attraction" created a seemingly insurmountable gulf.

Being near death softened mom's heart.

"I don't care about all that," she finally told me, "I just don't want anyone to hurt you. You need to be careful out there." She was frightened. She told me she was nervous that being an outspoken advocate would endanger my life. "I get it, Mom, but I'm ok. I'm really going to be ok."

Fear and hate are often mistaken for each other. Mom didn't hate me being gay, as much as she was scared for my well-being, and of course, my eternal salvation. And that was a distinction I didn't always understand.

At the end of her life we had achieved a reluctant détente—if not a deep acceptance. It was a time just before the arrival of Mormons Building Bridges and Mama Dragons, when coming out as an LDS parent of a queer child had an increasing number of support networks online. If she had held on a few more years, maybe she would have found a community of LDS parents in Oregon to bond alongside.

Maybe.

My dad and I though, were further apart. He was incredibly uncomfortable with homosexuality. He still would never publicly acknowledge the reality of a gay son. When the topic came up, he would bristle and swiftly change the subject.

Consequently we don't talk much about my life in Utah. I have a new boyfriend, Josh, who I'm crazy about. But they are not interested in hearing the details, nor are they curious about how we met. (Fun side note: it was at a kiss-in protest I was leading over the church's political activities. I needed someone to kiss, and he was the cutest in the crowd. Thank you Mormons!)

My family adopted a Don't Ask, Don't Tell policy with me, and as a result, they are not privy to my heart's greatest joy. Falling in love is ridiculous fun, and more so when you can gush about it with the other people you love.

My parents' left-leaning activist son is the political opposite of their daughter, Tammy, a happy-go-lucky extrovert who also champions conservative populist politics. She is even further to the right than my dad. And they argue ferociously about politics too. He just can't win with his kids.

I'm alone with my sister going through Mom's library of books. Tammy picks up a book she had gifted her.

"Troy, you should read Ron Paul's *Revolution*," Tammy tells me, "He speaks Truth."

"Sure," I pivot picking up the book I had bought for my Mom, "I'll read Paul if you will read Naomi Klein's *Shock Doctrine*. Deal?"

"I can never read a feminist," she responds. "I don't hate men."

"Wait, feminism does NOT mean that you ..."

Stop.

Just.

Stop.

We're at a standoff. Just keep the peace. This isn't about politics. It's all about Mom.

Thankfully, we've got the arrival of extended relatives to distract.

Aunts, uncles, cousins, and ward members stream through the front door at increasing intervals. I recommit myself to non-political, non-religious conversations. This will be a conflict-free reunion. My young nephews and nieces always provide a welcomed buffer. Somehow, despite growing up with staunchly conservative parents, they love their gay uncle without reservation. And I equally love them. The next generation of our family will not be like the last.

Then finally, by mid-afternoon, Elvis flies in from Orem.

He's in character and costume the moment I collect him from the Mahlon Sweet Airport. After thirty years performing as Elvis, this particular one has grown into the older, fatter variety of the King. The slick black hair and chops, the black jacket adorned with gaudy rhinestones. But also, a kind, generous smile. I grab his suitcase, and he responds with a familiar, "Thank you very much."

Oh boy.

We put the King up in my parents' guest room. Dad pulls out the

Elvis-themed pillowcases and duvet cover, as if they were bought and waiting for just this very moment.

Our esteemed guest is gracious and good-natured despite the jumble of bereaved mourners he's never before met. He spends the morning and evening humming "Love Me Tender" and "Don't Be Cruel"—all the hits. Not surprisingly, our conversation is dominated by Elvis trivia.

"Elvis had a passion for Gospel music," he expounds. "He earned a black belt in karate." He is indignant at the slights Elvis endured. "He made over thirty movies, but none of them ever won an Oscar. Can you believe that?" He shakes his head, incredulously. "Elvis wasn't a junkie as some have supposed. He only ever used prescription meds. He was only forty-two when he died." Later he mentions, "The Osmond Family gave Elvis a copy of the Book of Mormon that he treasured. I know he had a testimony, but circumstances wouldn't allow him to meet the missionaries." He shared this conviction with absolute certainty.

But our faux Elvis also had a canny ability to observe our tense family dynamics at play.

Sensing my discomfort with the ongoings, he quietly took me aside to share with me his personal story.

"My family rejected me," he quietly remembered. "My wife's father didn't want us together. He didn't believe I could make it as an Elvis. But ..." he leans toward me with deep earnestness, "I knew deep down inside that this is who I was supposed to be."

And then he winks, knowingly.

Oh my heck, am I bonding with a fat Mormon Elvis?

This is all so bizarre.

The evening before the celebration, our extended family and friends congregate in my parents' living room. We play polite catch up. The conversation is pleasant and anodyne. That is until our family friends Mel and Marjorie arrive from their ranch near Mount Hood. *Ok now, here we really go.* As far back as I can remember, Mel has been preparing his family for the collapse of the US government. Nineteenth-century Mormons were millenarians who believed the Second Coming was eminent—hence the "Latter-day" before "Saints."

There is still a fringe element within the church who believes the dreadful day is nigh. They hoard canned and freeze-dried food, semi-automatics, and gold. Mel and Marjorie are those very preppers. Mel tells me that their property sits adjacent to a secret US military facility housing UFOs. Mel explains, "We've seen several ones of 'em. Glowing lights just rise up and hover over our property, and then PHEEEW!" his arms darts upward, "they shoot right up into space! They know what's going on." I politely excuse myself to another room. But like a voyeur, I keep listening.

"I sure like that Glenn Beck," Mel tells Dad, and then later retorts, "What I can't stand is all the queers and their agenda. Jamming it down our throats"

Mel, do you even know how gay you sound?

My father doesn't respond. I'm waiting, hoping he will say something, anything to defend me.

He doesn't.

Really Dad? Nothing? I'm just resigned to it all.

Finally, it's evening. The Celebration of Life is about to begin at the senior center.

The crowd is strolling in.

Happy Anniversary Mom and Dad! Fifty years. We've gathered here to make merry.

Now, unbeknownst to me, Elvis had arrived earlier to set up his merch table. Yup. That's right. His merch table. I walk over to see exactly what he has on display. And that's when I see the stack of CDs and the sign:

"$10 EACH"

What!? I start to panic. *No! He can't do this. Not here!* Suddenly all the shame I felt as a kid living in mom's plastic Graceland swells up inside me. I pick up one CD with cover art of Elvis in the Celestial Kingdom kneeling before the Mormon Jesus.

"How Great Thou Art and other Elvis Gospel Songs as performed by…"

My anger builds.

Are you FREAKING KIDDING ME? Really?? This is g#@*mn tacky! *It's embarrassing! It's unrefined! It's almost … almost …*

Stop.

Just.

Stop.

Elvis is selling CDs at my mom's funeral.

How is that *not* awesome?

I laugh.

Somehow, my anger is instantly transmuted into loud laughter. And then laughter mixed with tears of joy. It's all absolutely absurd. Like a quirky dark comedy at Sundance. And I somehow have given myself over to it all.

And then it begins. The fluorescent lights above flicker. The unmistakable horns and pounding drums of *Also Sprach Zarathustra* build through the might of a tiny Casio Songstar karaoke machine.

The crowd of seniors cheer!

The King has arrived.

And wow. Elvis kicks off his set with "Suspicious Minds," segues into "Heartbreak Hotel," then brings the room down with "In the Ghetto." Hips thrust and gyrate through "Hound Dog" as he throws his sweat-drenched handkerchief to the purple-haired sisters, who hoot and holler.

He is … I have to admit … absolutely killing it. And I'm surprised to realize I'm grinning ear to ear.

The crowd continues to go wild, including, perhaps, my disembodied Mom, who I choose to believe is hovering right here, on the front row, dancing to the "Jailhouse Rock."

Her celebration is awesome.

On New Year's Eve, we drive to the Oregon coast to release my mother's ashes.

Not only did my mother not want a typical Latter-day Saint funeral, she also wanted to be cremated, which is a very not-Mormon thing to do. But she was pragmatic, and wanted her organs donated to science, and her ashes spread on the Oregon coast.

In her estimation, God was all powerful, and could easily restore her body together on the morning of the First Resurrection anyway. So, best not to get caught up in all the details. It was, for her, an act of perfect faith.

I was expecting that it would just be me, Tammy, and Dad. But then Elvis opened a fortune cookie the day prior that prophesied,

"You will visit an American coastline soon." My sister piped in, "Well, I guess that means you're coming with us."

I'm resigned. *Sure, of course, why not?*

The jetty in Florence is dangerously wet. The wind unrelenting. We arrive weary but brave. We walk out as far as we can safely manage. The umbrella is useless. We are quickly soaked and cold. Dad slips and falls on the large jagged black rocks. I help him up and in doing so, drop the box of Mom.

F*@k! Sorry Mom! Sorry! Grrrr. (I know I shouldn't curse in front of her.)

I'm frustrated, cold, and miserable. This isn't the way it's supposed to be. This can't be how we say goodbye.

Being the youngest, I climb down the slick black rocks to empty my mom's ashes into the ocean. I scale close to the lapping waves. *Isn't this all supposed to mean something more?* I breathe deep, then sigh hard, impatient and again, resigned.

Let's just do this.

And then, what do you know?

The wind and the rain subside so quickly and gently it feels not like a lull but a complete disappearance. Sun cracks through the sullen sky; the storm has just ...

Stopped.

Time stands still.

There is only my family and the ocean's roar.

Everything is peaceful and sublime. My numb fingers tear open the box and plastic to empty my mother's remains into the waters she loved. A few flakes cling to my fingertips, as her yellow ashes float atop the waves.

It's a perfect, sacred moment.

Mom is everywhere.

Like a river flows to the sea, darling, so it goes, some things are meant to be ...

After several timeless moments, the rain returns. Mom's ashes are absorbed into the majestic Pacific. And the sacred stillness is still resonating in my heart, warming my soul. We make our way carefully back to the car, wet but also joyful. I'm even growing ever fonder of this Elvis avatar in our company.

Of course Elvis would be here to send off Mom. *How could it be any other way?*

Driving back to Eugene, under the winding, towering moss-hung canopy of Douglas Firs, I reflect on my childhood shame of being working-class poor. I yearned for a life of high culture. Instead, Mom played Elvis records and immersed herself in romance novels. But also ABBA, Liberace, and the Village People (yes, I actually grew up thinking their song "Go West" was about Mormon Pioneers).

Looking back now, my childhood was all kinds of gay!

I've often thought that being queer is more than just a sexual orientation. For many it's also an exit strategy. Being gay rescued me from religion and the blue-collar kitsch I had long resented. Yet, weaving home through the night rain I feel for the first time a deep comfort with, and even gratitude for, all I ever wanted to escape.

Dad drives me to the Eugene airport the next morning. The Oregon sky is still damp and gray. He tells me that he fears the future alone. Little do we know that in four months he'll be remarried with a new wife. It's what Mormon widowers do. He hands me my suitcase.

"Troy, I'm … proud of who you are."

He still can't say the word "gay," at least not to me. I don't think he ever will. "I'm proud" is a catchall that acknowledges the unspeakable. For now, it's the best he can do. And I'm okay with that. Today, I can give him grace.

Through Mom's funhouse funeral, she has given me one final, lingering gift: a deep acceptance of everything I cannot change.

And I depart wondering if perhaps my need to be accepted by my family, also requires *that I accept them* in all of their eccentricities. My libertarian sister. My homophobic dad. And my new friend, Elvis. My backward Mormon American family.

Strangely, today, I can't help falling in love. With all of them.

Some things are meant to be.

HAVE NOT, HAVE KNOT

KEL PURCILL

"Keke," he says, one leg a staccato bounce at the corner of my sight. Brown eyes look up, fretful, wary, then morphing with a glitter of something hopeful. He calls me Keke, not auntie, not my legal name, but Keke—a nickname I was given in my teens by a best friend lost to time, somehow knotted into the now, into new connection and conversations.

"Keke ... you're not straight, are you." It's not a question. It's a confirmation, a quiet statement of fact.

I'm late forties, and this is the second time in my life someone in my family has asked this, and in this way. Something complicated knots and tangles in my throat, long threads unspooling through my ribs and giving a sudden, breath stealing yank.

You're not straight are you. The knots and ties keeping me tethered to the now unfurl, trailing clouds of glory until I come hard, hard against the past.

My mum's eyes look up, almost to my face, then away. Her hand shakes as she takes a final puff, fumbles the stubbing out and has to bend over to pick up the butt. Puts it in the bin. I can feel my right arm getting sunburned, my hands freezing as I stare at her, wondering why I thought she'd act differently. Mums are meant to, right? Be supportive?

"I like girls too, though. I do." Me, words rough, gnarled.

She shakes her head. Tiny, seismic motions.

She sighs, the nicotine scent familiar and obscene.

"No. You do NOT."

That was the one conversation I had with my mum about not

being straight. I was a teen, scared that I was somehow broken, but just like my allergies I couldn't just not be like that, and that was okay, right? Right?

Wrong.

I was not like that. The end.

She did say one other thing about that conversation, later that day. Mum came into my bedroom where I was poised like a wedge-tailed eagle above a rabbit, waiting with two suspended fingers to press REC:PLAY on my tape player when the music clip started on Countdown Revolution.

"Hey," she said, straightening an already perfect bedspread, "about what you said before."

Now I was the rabbit, frozen and sure something was hurtling towards me. Maybe something good?

Mum looked up, met my eyes. "Do NOT say that to your father."

Panic and roaring air, like I was both the plummeting eagle and clawed rabbit in one chaotic moment, utterly horrified at the idea.

I shook my head wildly, *no no no no WAY*, potential futures and damages spilling through my head like the guts from the rabbit in last week's science class.

"Not to anyone," she said after a beat, then turned and left.

I turned back to the tiny TV. Sat. Dimly heard Molly Meldrum say something about the next artist to take the world by storm … then the news was on and it was time for the weather. Where I was, both on the weather display and watching, was not visible on any map.

It's weird the ties that bind, the words and actions that sever connection.

"Keke … you're not straight, are you." It's not a question. It's a confirmation, a quiet statement of fact.

It's the second time someone in my family has asked me, not even asking, just a quiet recognition. The first, my youngest, barely two years ago before she turned twenty, and now my nephew in his mid-teens. I recognize he's chosen the moment to ask, too, with my mum just having gone inside to make us all cuppas, which guarantees a few minutes alone amid the climbing vines and dog's demands for belly scratches.

I grew up knowing, down to my bones, that mountains were the best, that you didn't mention any bruises or extra makeup you saw on women, that my dad didn't like me, and that being gay was the worst thing a guy could be.

"Is there gay ladies? What is gay?" I wasn't even seven, but I remember some questions were so utterly ignored I'd wake some nights afraid that I'd become invisible, just for asking them.

"What is what?" Aunt Mim asked me, leaning sideways to see what I was reading. She would actually talk to me, answer my questions, and she smelled amazing and was the most beautiful person I had ever seen. It was a family barbecue, lunch had been eaten, the adults all softened and hazy in the heat and their empty glasses, chatting about boring adult stuff.

"Gay—what is it? Is it like Italian or French? Where is it on the map?" I asked again, holding out my current fascination, a world atlas. I'd recently learnt from Mr. Lesniak that some countries in my atlas had changed names and the lines were borders but not walls, and that while he was from Poland his Chihuahua was from Mexico. Trying to work out how two creatures from pages apart in my book could somehow end up in my town together was one of several mysteries I was trying to solve.

"Is gay like Poland? Was it called something else?"

Mim was about to answer when my dad laughed. "Gay isn't a place, it's not on any damn map," he said, raising his beer.

"So not like Poland? Or how France people become French?" I asked.

"No, not like—" Mim started, but the questions would *not* wait their turn.

"What about gay ladies then? Are they a thing? Where are they? Did they have a country or were a bit of a country like Chihauhas?"

Somehow I'd caught everyone's attention. Maybe me, or it was Mim and Dad laughing at something funny and telling everyone how I wanted to know if gay ladies were Chihuahuas.

"So they're real?" I asked, patting at Mim's arm while everyone else was distracted, laughing, joking, getting more ice and drinks.

"Are what real, sweetie?" Mim asked. I was never invisible to Mim.

I leaned in close, sniffing at her perfume, then whispered "Gay ladies. They are real? Can you show me where?" I held the open atlas out again, a cheap, dog-eared expanse, offered like a sacrifice.

She took the atlas, lay it on her lap and smoothed out the pages. She didn't say anything.

"Mim?" I breathed, a wary eye on where Dad and Nan were, trying to get my answer before they interfered. "What's gay? Where is it? Dad said Bill is gay," Mim's eyes flick to our neighbor's house, "but he's nice, so why is gay bad?"

"KELLIE." It's a bark, loud and mean, snapping down the table. "Leave her be. Don't worry about gays. Bloody poofs," Dad growls, and before I can ask what Bill has to do with the big comfy cushions my nan has, Mim is passing me the closed atlas, kisses my forehead and pushes me gently towards the house.

"There's an Elvis movie on," she entices me. "Don't ask any more, okay? It's not ... good."

I take my questions and my atlas inside, where there is an Elvis movie on and while I find Hawaii on the map, then draw in some waves like in the movie, I never do find gay on the map.

Mim was right. Asking questions was not good.

"Your mum said you were looking into the family tree," Nan said, her morning glass of wine sweating in the tropical humidity. "I thought you might like this, was my uncle's."

I'm already reaching, not only because she's handing over the book, but because the effort of lifting it and holding it out is making her arm shake. She takes a mouthful of wine, lifts a hand to dab delicately at her mouth.

I turn it over, baffled by its leather cover. Actual, hand-tooled, stamped and aged leather. It's not professional binding, definitely domestic. That said, it's carefully done: the edges have tiny holes bored along the borders, a curled piece weaving through and around, hugging the entire book, front and back. Decorative stamps are pressed into the corners, filigree leaves and shaved angles, a polish leaving the entire case smooth and raspy. It's a tactile delight, and I'm surprised by more details the closer I look.

"That's my uncle's, he did the leatherwork himself. There was a whole bookshelf of leather-bound books he did. I've never read of them," she sniffs, disinterest plain—I've never seen Nan read anything more than a menu at a restaurant, "but you like books and family history. So. This one's yours."

She takes another drink, another dab to her uneven lipstick. "How about we go to the club for lunch?"

Nan chatters about what she had for lunch last time while I open the book. A page in and the publication date is … wow. Early '50s. A story of Saul and David. The magic scent of old paper and history, of a book I haven't read yet, a connection to a family member unmet and long gone, who obviously loved books like I do.

It's not until later—hours, and later again, years—that I realize Nan didn't tell me her uncle's name. It's not okay. It's not.

It's the second time someone in my family has asked me, not even asking, just a quiet recognition. The first, my youngest, barely two years ago before she turned twenty, and now my nephew in his mid-teens. I recognize he's chosen the moment to ask, too, with my mum just having gone inside to make us all cuppas, which guarantees a few minutes alone amid the climbing vines and dog's demands for belly scratches. And who doesn't appreciate some decent belly scratches?

Am I straight? I raise an eyebrow, something complicated twisting and tying in my chest and—looking straight at him—shake my head. Nope. His shoulders drop with his whooshed relief, for half a second his binder catching his t-shirt's material, then he bites his smile trying to keep everything low key.

"Definitely not." I squinch up my face, attempting straight thoughts, shake my head again. "Nope, not straight."

I read the book, enjoying the ripple of leather edging against my fingers, the musk of decades old paper and ink, the odd pacing and composition of the story. Saul was mighty, sometimes vicious, just, and noble. David was determined, hopeful, whole-hearted, a little naïve. They connected, tied close by responsibility, friendship, were better together, changed their piece of the world, each other's lives. It was not anything I'd not heard at church, not anything new even being thousands of years retold.

Then, deep within the embrace of the handcrafted cover, Saul and David loved each other. Knew each other, biblically, emotionally, physically, and again. A few pages later, a last kiss. No more than four paragraphs in hundreds of pages, but definite. Deliberate. Pressed like a kiss to a lover's secret places, gay love expressed, printed, read.

This was not just a book. Not an irrelevant family heirloom, casually passed unread for decades.

He had a whole shelf of leather covered books, Nan had said. A whole shelf.

Of handheld, hand-turned, pages and stories and then-unmentionable people and relationships and longings housed carefully, lovingly, one deliberate caress of hand and tool at a time, into personally crafted covers. Covers made of touch and tactile smoothness, of divots and twists, molded spine to fit in the palm, fingertips grazing random (*not random, oh hell and brilliance, not random!*) whorls and patterns. This was not a hobby, not some acceptable use of time and resources in something as close to art blokes of that time and place could sink into without censure, without fear.

This was hope. And loss. A whole shelf of can and cannots, right there and invisible, collected, protected, brave and brazen and—silent.

Something knotted in my throat, in my belly, in the domestic routine of woman-wife-mother. Something weaved, wefted and pulled, and as my fingers traced the fuzzy pages and raspy cover edges, the thought rose: I am—we—we are not the only one.

Not the only queerdo, weirdo, gay, not-straight in the family.

The leather groaned in my grip as I tried to absorb the magnitude of it … then I went to cut apples into slices, went back into my days, went back to being mostly as I was before. But not as the only queer in my family.

I did not tell my family—immediate, extended—what I had found in the pages. I agreed that it was a story of David and Saul, yes it was definitely different, yep it was not something I expected. What I really thought about the book was not my truth to tell … but was mine to hold. Safe keep.

It's weird the ties that bind, the words and actions that whisper and forge, layer and immerse in connection. I've lost the book (misadventure and unsupported queerness leading to its loss), but not what it's taught me, what it was like to be supported by people in my past, to have my own country called Not Alone.

Twenty years later, long divorced and still flirting with adding a dating app to my life, I'm building up my literature review for an advanced degree in queer studies. I want more details about that book I was given, lost, but have nothing close to enough to go on. Time to contact the one person who can help … which is a little problematic. Sadly, dementia has chewed on the edges of Nan, she who gave me the leather wrapped secret of family long gone.

Except, it turns out—not family? Maybe family? I asked Mim to ask some specific questions when she next visited Nan, now living in a nursing home and the past. Turns out the books were from Mark, the best friend of Da, Nan's dad. Mark, who was also a writer. And Mark did the covers himself. Either way, Mim relayed from Nan, the friend Mark gave the whole row of books to Da, who kept them, read them, never gave them on loan or away. Nan's not sure on many details but she remembers they were best friends, and there was a whole full row of leather wrapped books on Da's bookcase.

Does it matter who wrote the books, who created art to hold them, who gave them and read them? It does. And does not. It's poetic, really, that there was connection between Da and Mark, and the realities and ethereal detail of their relationship is lost to time except for the most important: they lived, they found each other, and they loved each other. Make of the possibilities what you will. Was every book a resting place of longing, of queer representation and recognition? Was it just this one book that was queer, the other tomes red herrings hiding the narwhal in their midst? Was the author a pseudonym of one of the men, of both? Was Da's home a refuge for Mark, for his books? Was Mark married? Was Da's wife—Nan's mother, my great-grandmother—aware of any or all of the knots and familiar grooves that made up Da and Mark's history and relationship, and what did that mean, and reveal?

It. Does. Not. Matter.

And it does.

And it doesn't.

More than anything, I am viciously, deeply, gleefully delighted, so hugely pleased that queers in the past, regardless of if they're related to me or not, had someone who knew them, protected them, valued and celebrated them. Even—especially—because I did not have that from my own family growing up, or now.

Last year saw the publication of a book with an essay I wrote about being queer—a piece knotted with melaleuca and paperbark, with history and blatant statement of my own queerness and sexuality. My mum read it—cracked the book wide open, lightning white now scarring down the spine, read it in the privacy of her own home. She's not said a word to me about it. Not a word. No recognition, no intimation. Not a thing. This does not matter. Not really.

Because.

Because there is a blooming, gorgeous satisfaction in being able to say "this is where I fit, this is how I belong" —especially in your own family. To be able to see connection, similarities, to raise worries and tend to dreams and not just highlighted differences and vast silences. Hopefully in our individual, historical families, or—failing our born or raised families' failure to provide comfort, love, and support—in our found and created families.

"Definitely not." I squinch up my face, attempting straight thoughts, shake my head again. "Nope, not straight."

We smirk at each other, eyes crinkling in the genetic lottery that won't let us hide our humor, roll our smiles between our teeth. We both look away, then back. I reach forward slowly.

We fist bump.

No. I'm not.

Because *oh* how my friends—my found family—danced at the news of my words made print. How they whooped and swore and sighed after reading it. How they came in close, held my face like the pages of a favorite book, familiar and beloved, eyes meeting mine, not content until the knots pulled us even tighter in, close enough to tangle and dig even deeper. *I see you. I love you. You are a country of welcome and brilliance, of comfort and weirdness. You are welcome here, where I am.*

Because in my secret, softest of hearts, I open the wonky door to an old house I've never seen, walk across to the bookcase, and run my fingers along the spines of an entire row of personalized, deliberately created and crafted books. At the end of the row there's a copy of the book with my essay in it, leaning against the worn leather of the one beside it, welcome and supported. I feel hands on my shoulders, and words soak like polish into my knotted, splintered heart: *We see you. We love you. We are so proud of you.*

Because when my youngest introduced herself to me when she was seventeen, it was to a country and immediate family of open arms and welcome, of kisses and support, of protection against extended family who would be cruel and uncaring, rude and refusing. When my nephew confirmed to himself that I was so not straight, it was into a world where there are out, unapologetic, queer supportive adults in his own family, not dead, not willing to shut up and NOT.

I did not have the answers as a child. I barely have answers to so many questions today. But I am not quiet about being queer, I am not silenced into professed straightness. I am not a place or person of danger to the queer people in my orbit, in my world, in my family, old and found.

I am not.

I am not going anywhere that says I am not.

I see you. I love you. I am country, a constellation, a universe of welcome and brilliance, of comfort and weirdness. You are welcome here, where I am, where I go.

I am here.

JOY IS NOT MADE TO BE A CRUMB

JENN LEE SMITH

Dear LDS Church,

You were there for my mother when I began life at four pounds, purple from the umbilical cord wrapped around my neck, father not there because of political turmoil. She said a prayer of thanks to heavenly father as she cradled the bundle of grape-colored joy, no larger than a winter melon. You provided a place of belonging and safety to balance the loneliness of new motherhood and the terror of not knowing if her husband will survive to see his firstborn. When he finally joined us, she packed us all up and left their humid island of Taiwan to begin a new life in the high Rocky Mountains, closer to you. They were overwhelmed by a new language and basic survival needs, confused and humiliated at times by the antagonism of your followers because of their foreignness. But she kept her vow to stay true to you and in return, you provided a template for living and surviving.

It's hard for me to distinguish my relationship with you outside of her experience. I was allowed to exist inside the four-cornered world she created for us. *The church promises the highest joy beyond measure*, she reiterated often to my father who was beginning to question. He leads a farmer's life, waking up daily at 4:00 a.m. to carefully tend to a variety of fruits and vegetables (star fruit, persimmon, bok choy, water spinach) growing in abundance on their American soil and of which he freely distributes to neighbors and friends. She is happy in your church founded on this land and I'm happy for her. I've met so many kind-hearted people within your eggshell-colored walls. You taught me about mainstream America while paradoxically existing as an Outsider yourself.

For as long as I can remember I've stood on the sidelines of the cultural hall banquet picking at scraps as everyone else feasted. I know now that I have always been worthy of the feast, but what I crave and what gives me sustenance is not here. Recently, I visited other places showing up as my queer self and was reminded that I am inherently deeply spiritual. It's okay that it took me this long to realize it. Every second I get to be myself is a sacred one.

I'm saying goodbye to you as a place of worship, a belief system, and the way of knowing myself and God. I am reconnecting with my spiritual self who never left me, always patiently asking, *what if joy really is that easy?* She's vibrant, creative, dynamic, and curious about people and the world. She celebrates humanity and all that we are as part of all that lives and has ever lived. She recognizes that we forget the light inside because of our need for belonging. My spiritual practice reflects my values of listening to my body and of living in harmony with Mother Earth.

My body feels lighter as I've listened to its needs, as I've given voice to my wounded child—who is queer. I'm walking a new path away from religious institutions and filial piety. Most nights, I do meditation for ancestral healing. Once, my ancestors stood together and playfully chided me for sometimes doubting this new path, one they would have chosen for themselves if given the choice. *Don't fuck this up*, they said. *But no biggie if you do.*

Last summer in the forest, I gathered with my chosen family, seated on logs facing each other instead of in pews facing forward. We hike, we forage, we feast, and we leave a place better than we found it. At first, I often had to step away in disbelief that such expansion and love is possible. With each new joyous celebration, whether it's creating a colorful mural of a tree out of origami originally designed by a family member or singing carpool karaoke with my children, I am learning to be unafraid of plenty.

If you suddenly and unexpectedly feel joy, don't hesitate. Give in to it [...] Joy is not made to be a crumb —Mary Oliver

THE TREE OF LIFE
HAS MANY BRANCHES

CONNOR DAVIS

April 6, 2022

I feel empty.

The grayness is creeping and seeping. I'm not worried, however. I've been here before. The gray is a regular patron, and I've witnessed much darker and harsher anyways. In comparison, it feels familiar … almost comfortable.

Deep breath. Sigh.

I swing my legs over the edge of my mattress and feel the lead of my feet hit the floor. I press the heels of my hands into my eye sockets and rub away the sleep. What's left of it anyways, I never get much these days.

Deep breath. Deeper sigh. A twinge deep in my chest.

The pain of grief begins clawing at my heart as the grogginess slips from my brain and memories of *her* flood my consciousness.

One foot in front of the other. One day at a time, I tell myself. The usual cliché bullshit we all cling to at times. I currently have white knuckles.

It's been about a month since she and I have seen each other … or talked. Much longer since the breakup. We were never married, so it can't be called divorce. But ripping someone out of your life after they've been there day in and out for years? Breakup is a flimsy ass word.

But I trudge on. Something I wasn't entirely capable of on my own before I met her. She taught me things, whether through causing me pain or healing my pain (you can understand why things ended). She taught me a lot about life and happiness and navigating my emotions. She taught me about the trudging I had already done. Showed me my strength. My resilience.

So despite my current emotional state, I have hope for the future. My phone vibrates.

My legs push me off the floor of my mind and I swim up out of the depth of my thoughts and back to reality.

Twitter notification.

I unlock my phone and open Twitter. It's a DM. From a mutual follower (we follow each other).

Her profile photo is tiny and her handle isn't instantly familiar. I immediately click onto her profile page to do some stalking.

She's gorgeous! Holy shit, she messaged me first?! Am I dreaming?!

I respond. My hands clam up.

Her name is Keeli. She's pan. She's polyamorous! She's married …!?

April 30, 2022

Getting to know Keeli is amazing. Flirting gives me swarms of butterflies. She's witty, she's soft, she's unbelievably healthy and secure. But I don't really want or need a relationship right now. Besides, I'd always imagined myself having a nesting partner, my person, and feeling secure with them before stepping out into full-on polyamory.

But of course, she doesn't mind. She's happy to embrace the dynamic nature of a flirtationship. We mutually enjoy each other's company. Friendship is *plenty*, and I'm glad to have her. And while I hate the serving of cheese this statement is, she just *gets* me.

May 13, 2022

We just finished reading *Alone with You in the Ether* by Olivie Blake. My ex wasn't much of a reader. Keeli is.

The story was fascinating, and also eerily relatable. We see ourselves in the characters. The willingness to embrace chaos. The unwillingness to medicate against inner chaos for fear of dulling the experience. The gray feeling of being a messy, imperfect human falling in love with another equally messy human. Handling the grief of not having made different choices or missing out on a different life. The book says we live in a multiverse, where we navigate the various paths of reality with our choices.

We both grew up LDS and subsequently left the church. Her after marriage and kids. Me after my mission and a few semesters of college.

We talk at length about who we'd be now if our upbringing were different. We commiserate and grieve together about childhoods that didn't have to be so hard. We wonder about the possibilities and implications of destiny and personal purpose.

I'm dissociating. My mind traverses the multiverse ignoring any unpleasant sensations or emotions, just as I've done since childhood. Then suddenly a sound comes screaming from the depths of space. It's Rocket, my dog, whining to get into my room. I'm officially out of my reverie. Forced to face the knots in my chest and stomach. I get off my bed and let Rocket in. He takes a seat next to me and I scratch his head while I pick up my phone.

I message her, "Thinking about my childhood makes me feel like an angry kid. It's not my fault I wasn't given good emotional regulation skills. Negative emotions were seen as evil and meant to be repressed. Sadness was bottled. Rage was canned. Conflicts were met with the abrasive singing of hymns."

"Love at Home" begins to play in my ears like air raid sirens. I'm back in the trenches. But I know how to fight this time, so I march on with my questions. Facing the pain and confusion of being a human with opposing emotions and a gray-filled past. Rocket senses my unease and nuzzles my hand, a polite request for *more scratches, please.* But also maybe a *you aren't alone.*

I absentmindedly oblige and continue typing, "And where were all the people who were trained to recognize ADHD in children? I wouldn't have dropped out of college if I had been diagnosed and supported! And it frustrates me that you seem to be able to just accept that about yourself when I can't. What's wrong with me?"

She replies, "It's okay to be an angry kid. There's nothing wrong with feeling." I look down at Rocket and somehow know his eyes are saying the exact same thing.

My eyes burn. This must be unconditional love.

July 5, 2022

Keeli and I officially adopt titles as boyfriend and girlfriend. Her as the girlfriend, me as both depending on the weather. You feel me?

She's in Utah. We're meeting in person for the first time!

We've read a few more books together and spent countless hours video chatting or texting. We've even adopted virtual dates as a regular part of our relationship. Our communication is amazing. I feel safe. I feel secure. But the thought of meeting her isn't butterflies. It's a stampede of bus-sized wildebeests.

What if she thinks I smell weird? What if she doesn't like the way I stick my tongue out when I focus or think? What if the spark doesn't transfer to the physical realm? Oh god, she's staying at my house for multiple nights and she's gonna end up hating it and it's gonna be so awkward, and what if—

zzt zzt

She's here.

I swing the front door open. I step into the sun. She's stepping out of her car. We're always so in sync like this. How cute of us. We approach each other.

"Oh my god, Hi!" she beams a smile my way.

"Hiiiii, is this real? Are *you* actually real?"

"Yes, come here!"

The distance between us finally closes as I slip my arms around her waist. The wildebeests threaten to break out. I take a deep breath, unsure if there's enough oxygen in the atmosphere to calm me down. And then her smell. *Wow.* Sweet, woody, comfortable.

I feel the moment ending and we pull apart a bit to see each other's faces. The wildebeests move to my head. Are we gonna kiss? Is this just, like, a moment to savor?

"What do you want to do today?" she asks.

"I have no idea. I can hardly think or breathe. Maybe let's head inside and get you settled first?"

She chuckles, "Oh, thank God, I'm not the only one swimming in butterfly soup."

The next few days were a hazy cascade of tumbling skin and opening hearts. Late-night conversations and confessions.

Then she was gone.

July 28, 2022

My gray friend is back. I'm not sure it ever truly leaves.

I stare through my phone screen, dissociating as I scroll through Reddit. A notification. It's Keeli.

"Hey, I'm free right now until like 7, sooooo …"

She wants to video chat. I'm iffy. I look back at my gray friend.

I call her.

"Hey, hi, hello! I missed you!" the words shoot out of her mouth.

"Hi, I missed you," I mumble.

She can sense its presence. We sit in silence for a while.

"Do you ever think about how we don't force people to do things they don't like until it comes to the topic of life? And if you don't enjoy it, there's something wrong with you," I ask.

"I've never considered that. No. But that sounds hard to go through, I'm sorry."

Rage sparks within me. *If you're so sorry and claim to care at all, then give me answers or fix it.*

"I'm sorry to just dump my sad vibes onto you. I think maybe some people inherently don't enjoy life the same way some people don't enjoy chocolate ice cream. I think I'm some people."

"That's okay, I don't need you to change. I love you how you are."

I feel stinging in my tear ducts. How does she *do* that?

"God, and now I feel like shit because I come here giving you problems you didn't ask for and then harbor anger and resentment when you don't give me what I want. Baby, you deserve better. I don't want to hurt you and I don't know how to handle these feelings. It's the angry kid all over again, except now that you're closer to me I'm comfortable taking it out on you when you don't understand my screaming and whining."

She thinks for a bit.

"They're just thoughts and feelings, baby. And in the end, I know my own limits. Also? I trust you."

Her face on my screen blurs with tears.

She adds quietly, "I'm not scared of you."

That's it, I'm crying.

How did I ever get so lucky? Where was *this* love all my life? A love that's synonymous with acceptance. Total, undeniable acceptance.

I'm loved for who I am at my deepest parts, even if she'll never know them fully. But she's willing to try.

"I love you."

"I love you too. So much," and I don't doubt what she says one single bit.

January 5, 2023

It's almost been a year since "that fateful day." I've experienced a love and a joy I had never thought possible. Something truly enriching. Catalyzing.

Growing up I always felt "softer" than most boys. Keeli loves that about me. And while I may struggle to feel my feelings nowadays (due in no small part to having mastered the art of emotional canning), or struggle with feeling them overwhelmingly, she's been with me. Providing consistent and fearless love that has changed my views about the world and myself.

We are a small, self-aware, human-shaped part of the universe. The universe is inherently chaotic. So are we.

With so much unknown it's impossible and futile to plan an exact future that will be your happily ever after. Rather, the best we've got is to acquire some useful tools and friends along the way. Everyone's journey is unique, as are the ways to navigate it.

So, my toolkit for combatting the gray? Radical honesty with yourself and in your communication with others. To whatever extent you see fit. Radical acceptance is the cousin of radical honesty. Control only serves to increase your awareness of the chaos and how little control you actually have. Instead, we can learn to find beauty in the disorder, and gain an appreciation for the infinitude of entirely unique and personal experiences you or anyone has.

Keeli taught me these things.

Keeli's willingness to face the unknown head-on and to find joy in the journey has been a safe and healing place for me.

My journey away from Mormonism and into myself is a queer journey. To me, that means it will remain forever undefined. It's that exact chaos in myself that I'm learning to embrace. And just like the infinitely branching realities of our choices, there are a lot of unknowns. That means we'll *never* know how many branches lead us to inner peace and happiness. Maybe because the number of branches that lead you there is infinite.

SUMMER OF THE MOTHS

ALLYSON VERONA TURNER

To M

April

We are bound to each other by the sharing of our joys.

"How do you feel about Mary Oliver?" the message read.

I laughed. Oh, this woman was in for a treat. I'd made sure to mention poetry in my app profile because it's essential to who I am, but Mary Oliver is my all-time favorite poet. I've had her "Wild Geese" memorized since I first read it in college, so I told her as much.

"What's your ideal first date?" was next. I replied, describing the ideal picnic, in a world where the grass is properly comfortable and ants never spoil the scene.

"But a cute coffee shop is definitely a close second lol," I added.

The spring morning was clear and full of sunshine; the cafe we chose close enough for me to walk to and enjoy the changing of the seasons. I arrived first and selected a table in the back corner, the perfect place to keep an eye on the front door and soothe the butterflies of anxiety in my body. She also showed up early, carrying purple irises in one hand.

She didn't seem to either see or recognize me, so I shot her a quick text: "Hey, I got here early to do some work. I'm in the back corner, by the couch." Seconds later, we were making small talk, laughing about our mutual awkwardness. We shared our coming out stories, our similarly religious upbringings, and consequent faith transitions.

"What was it like growing up Mormon?" she asked.

"Well …" I hesitated. "It was good … and it was really difficult, but it shaped me into who I am today. I'm lucky to have great parents who taught me to love others. And, because I grew up in New Mexico, where we weren't the majority religion, well, that helped because I was constantly surrounded by people with different life stories and backgrounds than me. I was raised to appreciate that. I'm so glad my parents didn't raise me in Utah, that would have been … much less nice. But also, I gave a lot of my time and energy to church stuff growing up. I mean, three hours of church every Sunday, midweekly youth activities, annual local and general conferences, summer events. Not to mention leadership and activity planning meetings because I was always in leadership roles. It was a lot. I gave my all to the church and got my soul crushed in return."

"Wow. That is a lot."

"Yeah. Clearly, I'm doing great. What was it like for you, growing up Evangelical?"

And that's how our conversation would go. She'd ask an excellent question, obviously prepared ahead of time with thought and care, I would answer in detail and then ask the same question back to her. I could have sat and talked like that with her forever. Or at least long into the afternoon.

Coffee turned into breakfast turned into dinner and drinks turned into museum visits and movie nights and long talks about our pasts, our present, the future. My heart grew delicate wings and fluttered, dancing around the light radiating from her. The summer lay ahead of us, full of possibilities and magic.

I'm not very good at joy; it's not an emotion my body knows how to feel. Loud emotion is too much for my fragile body to carry. I like quiet emotions: peace, serenity, blissful happiness filling up my being the way a fresh mug of tea warms my hands on an autumn evening. I like to sit in silence and watch the sunset over the trees, the clouds change color and shape with the wind, the bats come out to weave their music across the twilight sky. I like moments where I can forget everything else—moments of distracted bliss.

June
If wickedness never was happiness, then happiness never could be wickedness.

Drunk on summer heat and the inevitability of our own youth, we gathered to dance and revel in our own beauty—friends and lovers, family and new acquaintances, all awash in the glow of Pride. Rainbows rippled over everything I could see from the train station to the streets of downtown Denver to the capitol building, its golden dome gleaming in the summertime sunshine. Like moths drawn to electric lights, we followed those rainbows all the way to the festivities, never needing to ask for directions. Our hearts knew the way.

She wore a black top, denim shorts, and a red scarf in her short black hair that reminded me of Rosie the Riveter, a much more sensible outfit than my thrifted white dress with the skirt dyed into a rainbow. At least the boots she lent me were practical. Our friends joined us, all sporting various staples of queer fashion—patterned button-down shirts, pride pins, glitter on our faces.

At the end of the walk downtown, I felt like Dorothy stepping into a Technicolor world for the first time—marveling at the amounts of rainbow, lashings of glitter, and abundances of every color imaginable that unfurled in all directions. Our contributions of color added to the festive atmosphere.

My heartbeat took on the rhythm and flow of the crowd circling its way around the booths and displays. The rhythm and flow of the music beating from every corner, the dancing matching in time. Rhythm and flow of our intertwined hands, keeping us together as we joined the crowd. Of our laughter mingling with the sunlight beaming, bending its way through the trees.

Maybe this is heaven? I thought. *Or part of it, at least.*

Stolen kisses, sweet as sugar, melted on my lips in the blazing sun, in the heat from all the bodies swarming around us. My heart began to settle down, a moth resting in the candlelight glow of midsummer, as my head rested on her lap and I looked into her dark eyes. The world is big enough for all our love.

In the late afternoon, my head felt strange; I reached up to my ears. In my memory, at this moment, something happens to the light. Something changes.

"Oh no! Baby, look," I said.

"What is it?" she asked. She couldn't tell that anything was different with me.

"I lost my earring. It must have come off somewhere."

"Do you want to look for it?"

"Yes, please. Like, it's okay if we can't find it, but I want to try." We scoured the ground we had recently covered, looking for a sign of the opalescent full moon whose twin sat in my left ear.

I never did find that earring. Its loss is not one I feel keenly; in fact, it only reminds me of that one exquisite day.

A dense fog covers my memories—fog formed through time and pain and the slipperiness of my mind. But when my people remind me in small ways that I am worthy of being loved, my heart bursts open like a dam and joy pours through my veins. The fog over my past doesn't dissipate, but it matters less because my future is a boundless sea of light and possibilities and love.

September
"There are no holy people or holy places, only holy moments."

It ended the way the best things end, all bittersweet and tender. Our paths crossed for a season, then diverged on an autumn evening. The full moon watched us tenderly, witnessing heartfelt words and tears.

I knew it was coming. I always know it's coming. The flame had been sputtering, my heart once again feeling unsettled and uncertain. Just like the short life span of the adult Luna moth, who lives only to love and die, the summer was coming to an end.

We never said the words *break up* but we both knew they hung heavy in the air between us when she said, "I think we both know what needs to happen now." When I didn't apologize for not being able to be anyone other than my truest self. When we kissed goodbye.

I did not tell her what I wanted to then, so I am doing it now.

Thank you. Thank you for loving me and showing me how to love myself. Thank you for nudging me out of my comfort zone while respecting my need to have one in the first place. Thank you for romanticizing my life and enjoying my perpetual optimism. Thank you for the art, the music, the flowers. Thank you for sharing your dark days with me. Thank you for crying with me. Thank you for cooking with me and for feeding me. Thank you for giving me space, for making me laugh, for making me cry. Thank you for allowing me to love you. I will always remember you fondly.

———————

I spent too many years convinced I would never find anyone capable of loving me in all my messiness, my queerness, my sickness, my paradoxical state of having so many emotions and hardly showing them. I may be too much for some, too little for others, unable to settle for anything less than unique. But I will always be enough for myself. I will rest in my own soul's glow.

SECTION 2

JOY IS DEFIANCE
AND FAITH

TO DANCE IN THE DIM LIGHT: MEDITATION ON JOY, PART 2

KERRY SPENCER PRAY

My children were still practically babies when I lost a quarter of my skin.

Most of it to infection, the rest to prevent a cancer from spreading.

Late in the summer of 2012, I was admitted to the burn ICU within minutes of my temperature spiking, just as the infection was entering my bloodstream.

I'd gone for a checkup with my oncologist. I knew I wasn't healing well. That my graft had failed, much more catastrophically than my last graft had. There was a fetid stench coming from my wound vac. No one could stand to be in the room with me, the smell of decay was so strong. My doctor had scheduled me for another surgery in a week.

During the oncology appointment they wheeled me into the office because I couldn't walk. My nurse had never met me. She was new to the office. She said hello and then she looked at me.

I remember the way she looked at me.

She got quiet.

She took my temperature. It was normal. She took my blood pressure. It was normal.

"Something is wrong," she said, out loud. "Something is more wrong than they think." She looked at me for one second, two seconds. "I'm going to make a phone call."

There was nothing to indicate she was right. No signs. Nothing that could be marked on a chart. She had instinct, alone.

But she made a phone call, and I was taken to the burn unit for a consult.

Sepsis has a 50 percent mortality rate.

And I arrived in the burn ICU *minutes* before I had any signs of it.

The Apocryphon of John is a Sethian Gnostic text written sometime before 180 CE. It has a version of the Garden of Eden that reads quite a bit differently than the traditional version of the Garden story, though it overlaps in interesting ways from the Mormon version.

Yaltabaoth, child of Sophia become demon, declares himself the One and Only True God and demands everyone must conform to his dictates. He makes a world that is neither light nor dark. It hovers in the in-between space. The fae gloaming, where fear is important, and fearing the One True God, is the most important.

In the tepid half-light of the dim world, Yaltabaoth creates Adam.

And through a trick, Sophia, one of the higher gods, blows her divinity into Adam.

Yaltabaoth is horrified, frightened of this creature who has the light of Sophia inside him. He creates a prison for Adam: Eden.

Sophia and the higher gods conspire to save Adam from the prison of Eden. They send him Eve—a helpmeet not because she belongs to Adam, but because she has the power to free him.

The Mormon story doesn't paint God as the villain—not quite—but Eve is still the hero. God's double bind of the garden—don't eat the fruit, multiply and replenish—meant that she could not keep the law without breaking it.

Adam fell that men might be.

Men are that they might have joy.

I spent a month in the burn ICU, and I think almost died.

I'm still not entirely sure what happened.

Maybe it was one of the medications I was on. Maybe it was a hypnogogic hallucination. Maybe it was a dream. Maybe it was something else.

I was unconscious, I knew I wasn't breathing. I could hear the beeping of a machine outside of me. Knew, in the way you know when you are not quite awake and still frozen in the paralysis of sleep, that I couldn't make myself breathe, even if I wanted to.

The air around me got cold.

There were stars and quiet and motion.

I moved through a wind.

There was a woman waiting for me, surrounded by rocks and earth and sky.

She wasn't beautiful. I'm not even sure she was human. But she was kind.

She took my hand.

"Kerry," she said. "Your mother gave you so many gifts."

I knew it was true.

I didn't know if the woman holding my hand was my mother, or if she spoke for her, but I knew I'd been given so many wonderful things. So many blessings, hidden somewhere underneath the yearning I never understood.

She touched my hair. "So do you know what you're supposed to do now?" she asked.

I didn't know. Didn't even know how to ask.

She smiled at me. "*You dance,*" she said.

I took a breath, heard a beeping, and I opened my eyes.

Coming back from near-death was slow and didn't involve very much (any) dancing. The grafts were stubborn and couldn't heal in the high altitude of Utah. Getting the wounds to close took years and a move to sea level.

I wrote an essay about running once, while I was immobilized, trying to get my grafts to heal. I wrote about the feel of the rhythm, hitting the ground with my feet. Breath in, breath out. It wasn't joy, and it wasn't dancing. But it was quiet. The feeling of motion I could never quite touch because motion does not help struggling skin grafts to close.

I don't know why I wrote the essay.

I missed motion. I wanted to dance, like I'd been told to. But I didn't know how. I only knew how to run from the ache I felt. The need that I would reach for and never understand.

The odd sense that things would always be wrong until I let myself accept something I did not want to accept.

I decided to leave the Mormon church in the bathtub.

There was a tree outside, and she would rock in the wind. Taller than my second-floor window by double, I watched the squirrels run up and down the branches. Woodpeckers, demolishing the bark with their brightly throated beaks. The frantic chirping of the birds punctuated the rustle of the leaves in the trees. The squirrel and woodpecker and tree and wind all had a rhythm. They didn't have to try. It wasn't hard for them. They just … danced.

I had decided years before that if I ever had a queer child, I would leave the church. I would do it immediately and without question. There was no room in the church for a queer child, and I could not imagine smothering a child that way, forcing them to stay in a place that hurt them, that told them over and over that they were broken and sinful and wrong and that their only hope was happiness in the next life, their only salvation in keeping that deepest part of them— the very divinity Sophia blew into them—quiet.

A crash of thunder made me stand up in the tub. I stood there, in the water, for a moment. I watched the storm, letting its energy fill my body. Letting the yearning be filled up with the rain and wind and leaves and creatures who knew how to dance.

I had been a queer child, I realized.

I had been a queer child and it had never, until watching that storm, occurred to me that I should leave the church for myself.

The moment—the very moment—I had the thought, I felt the church fall completely away. I felt Father God go quiet, watching. He didn't reproach. He didn't scold. But even if he had, it wouldn't have changed anything.

John's Eve wasn't born knowing that she had to break the law to save Adam. She was born in the dim world, like all of us. She was told the rules, like all of us. And she chose to break them. Because the point of it all, the purpose in her imprisonment, was to give the children of men the chance to dance in the dim light, to cry out in the morning dawn, to realize: divinity can be contained by no law, no false god, no dictate, no ideology.

Joy comes from recognizing the divinity inside you, her story says.

Joy comes from breaking the law in order to keep it.

I saw her again then. The flash of a shadow I sometimes saw on the back of my right eye.

She was smiling at me.

Dance, I felt her smile. *You were meant to dance.*

ASHES TO AUTHENTICITY

LAURIE LEE HALL

This essay is an excerpt from the author's upcoming memoir

"A massive fire destroyed the Provo Tabernacle, a historic building that has been a landmark in Provo for more than a century."

December 17, 2010, is a day I'll never forget.

It was a wintry day; I had taken time off work. My wife at the time, Marleen, and I were driving to Snow College in southern Utah to pack up our daughter Liz, who had just completed her associate degree. Liz was leaving in January to serve an eighteen-month mission at the Los Angeles Temple Visitors Center.

As we neared Salt Lake City, I received an email on my cell phone from the Church Office Building where I worked, indicating the Provo Tabernacle had experienced a fire. We turned on KSL News-Radio and heard the shocking news, beginning with the byline above.

"What do you suppose happened?" Marleen asked, guessing I might know something.

"I really can't imagine." Thinking of my colleagues in the Meeting-house Facilities Department who had stewardship over the building, I thought aloud, "I hope this wasn't a mistake on MFD's part."

Curiosity got the better of me, so on our way south we stopped in Provo. Of course, it was not permitted, nor wise, to get too close to the tabernacle. Heavy, dark smoke was still rolling forth into the sky above downtown.

"Did you ever attend meetings there when you were at BYU?" I asked Marleen.

"We had a stake conference there, and a Christmas concert right around this time of the year, just before the semester let out," she replied.

"From what I'm seeing, the Tabernacle could be completely destroyed."

We continued to Snow College where we packed up Liz's things. The next morning, we went with Liz to the Manti Temple so she could receive her own temple endowment rites before she left on her mission.

Our time in the temple the next morning with Liz was delightful. As was often the case, I was as focused on the historic murals and architectural details as much as I was on the sacred religious ceremony. The temple was not busy, so after the ceremony, one of the temple workers escorted us on a relaxed tour of the rest of the venerable building.

The previous month, I had a stomach virus and my health rapidly deteriorated. Unable to keep anything down for several days, I became dehydrated and realized my bowels were not moving. What followed was excruciating pain that forced me into the local hospital, where I remained for four days. The doctors could find nothing wrong with me and sent me home without answers.

Back home, I attempted to eat to regain my strength and was punished with severe abdominal pain. The next day was our stake conference and I was serving as stake president. I arranged for my counselors to cover the afternoon meetings, but I dressed and attended the evening adult session, where I was scheduled to speak.

Sitting on the stand as the presiding officer, I was in agony. When it came time to speak, I stood and held white-knuckled to the pulpit, resting my forearms upon it to maintain my balance, cramping so severely I thought I might pass out. Such was my devotion to my church service. When it was over, I was satisfied that I had given my full measure of strength to accomplish my assignment.

The next day my condition had worsened. We decided I needed to go to the Intermountain Medical Center in Salt Lake City.

"We're not sure what's going on, but we're going to start you on an NG Tube." It meant nothing to me, but unlike the hospital back in Lincoln, they were taking some action. "We'll just insert this tube into your nostril and down your throat into your stomach so we can completely empty you out. As you feel it enter your throat, try to swallow several times, that will help lead it down."

I tried to hide my terror with a joke, "Then I suppose NG stands for 'No Good,' right?" The nurse claimed I took it well, but the insertion made me gag; it was horrible.

For the next five days I was confined again to a hospital bed, this time attached to an IV and with the NG tube linked to a vacuum line that removed the entirety of my stomach and upper intestines' contents into a quart-sized clear canister mounted on the wall above my bed. A nurse came to record its volume and general appearance from time to time. At first the canister was filled with the most garish colored thick sludge imaginable, but in time ran almost as clear as the IV fluids I was receiving.

"We cannot see anything on the scans we've performed, other than your colon tissue. There is no physical blockage. Our hunch is that your colon simply collapsed. We won't know for sure unless we take a look via surgery. First, let's wait a few days and keep you emptied out, then perhaps the colon will relax and open back up on its own."

That was the best these doctors had. I needed to stay put and give it time. So, I was left to rest, to think, and contemplate if surgery was my next step.

I thought a lot. I decided I would be the most thankful and cheerful patient I could, despite my circumstances (I had not been so positive while in the previous hospital, which I regretted). I have always believed though we seldom can choose our challenges, we are free to choose how we respond to them. Finding myself as miserable as I think I have ever been, I knew I needed to choose to be the kindest and most patient person I had ever been.

———

The Monday following the Provo fire brought surprising news. The Presiding Bishopric, temporal affairs leaders of the church, asked my work group, not Meetinghouse Facilities, to take stewardship of the remains of the tabernacle, stabilize what was left, collaborate with city officials, and determine if the building could in any way be saved. The assignment made sense. A few years earlier we led the reconstruction and seismic stabilization of the Salt Lake Tabernacle on Temple Square. I felt a thrill and a sense of confidence to work on another iconic historic building.

In 2004 when I'd been asked to oversee the renovation of the Salt Lake Tabernacle, I was not confident. It seemed that there was a much higher chance of it being a career-ending project than a career-building one.

This time would be different.

Having decided to be completely gracious while I endured the NG tube, I spent the next several days peeling the onion of my attitude toward everything. Perhaps I realized if I could choose in these extreme circumstances to be my best self, I could also commit to doing so each day going forward. My task became clear before me: I needed to identify and remove all harmful elements of my character—while safeguarding the good—and perform a deep assessment of whatever should be repaired, strengthened, or even rediscovered.

I had time and space while confined to bed to conduct a thorough look inward. There was a lot about myself I did not like. I had to admit I was often angry, prone to speak harshly, to be unduly demanding, generally ill at ease with myself and others, and frankly without peace. I reflected on the many times I had treated others poorly.

I could not have known at that time in the hospital bed, connected by the NG tube to the goop-filled canister, where my self-assessment would take me. When healing came and I was pronounced free to leave, I went home only with the conviction that changes had to come. I committed to finding the root causes behind my untoward demeanor and to do the work to become a new me and to live in peace. I was ready, if necessary, to burn down any part of my life. Should I have been asked at the time, I would not have been able to say who or what the new me was. I am unsure I would have had the courage then to say it even if I had known it.

Within days of the fire, our construction personnel had erected the scaffolding-like framework to stabilize the brick walls of the Provo Tabernacle. Just a shell of the building was all that remained. There was legitimate concern any seismic movement or strong winds could cause even more to be lost. Once the walls were stabilized, various teams could go to work to investigate the remains. The Provo City Fire Marshal's office would search for the cause of the fire, and the insurance adjusters were anxious to know the extent of the loss. Our team was hopeful to salvage and document any details that might exist to aid the design process. Historians were desperate to observe what they could before more of the building was lost. The public clamored for answers and any news from the church regarding what would become of the beloved building. Church leaders anticipated our team's report on the viability of reusing the building. For many months all eyes were trained on our every activity.

My first walkthrough of the remains of the tabernacle came on a frigid, bright morning just after the New Year. I saw the building in ruins. The fire began in the attic structure, causing the roof to collapse down through the perimeter walls and crushing the mezzanine balcony, organ, and rostrum below. A beautiful and sacred building, now hollow, had been all but lost.

The winding stairway in the southeast corner turret was the only one of the four still usable, so we ascended it and looked out across the scene from what would have been the attic access door. The smoldering debris had been soaked with hundreds of thousands of gallons of water for several days following the fire. January's freezing temperatures turned the debris pile into a solid block of muddled ice ten to twelve feet thick. Deep within the ice lay the answers to all the questions we were seeking.

In 1996, before moving my family to Utah to work at church headquarters, a friend suggested I read the paperback self-help book *What Color Is Your Parachute?* From it I learned the benefit of stepping back to identify what brings joy, fulfillment, or satisfaction in employment. I understood how the same principles applied to other aspects of life. As 2011 began, I undertook to find or rediscover those things in my life that brought me peace and joy.

Journaling helped me recognize things about myself that felt wrong, such as how I dealt with conflict or pressure, which I believed were unhealthy and needed to be mitigated. I began looking deep into the contents of my shell to discover what should be kept and what could be built upon. Always there, just below the surface, was my female gender identity. I convinced myself for three decades that my awareness of being female had successfully been buried. Given the life choices I made as an adult over that time, it appeared I had no option but to continue to conceal what seemed forbidden to ever be a part of me.

I decided to use my scarce spare time to start writing a "fictional" narrative. The protagonist was a talented young woman designer named Laurie Corridoio. When I worked for an Italian family during high school making pizzas, their nickname for me was Corridoio, Italian for hallway. The story unfolded with many details of Laurie's childhood and teen years with family, followed by college and young adulthood. Although I pretended I was writing fiction, several chapters in I admitted to myself I was writing my own story from the perspective of having lived it as Laurie. Through new eyes, I realized that young Laurie's life was so much happier than mine had been, even though many of the details were the same. She grew up free from the sadness and anxiety of hiding her true self and struggling with constant gender conflict. I envied her peace.

By writing the narrative, I inadvertently exhumed my female gender identity from being secreted away, laid it bare in front of me, and walked in her shoes for several months as she (I) told her story. The toothpaste had left the tube and it wasn't going back. I felt a peaceful connection to Laurie. This female identity I then knew so little about seemed to be the new me I was seeking. Around May 2011, I gave myself permission to dive into understanding who I really was, who I needed to be.

—————

After five months of investigation, the Provo Tabernacle team had completed their assessment and report. I submitted the results to the Presiding Bishopric to present to the First Presidency. We reported the building was not a total loss, but was salvageable and could be preserved in similar fashion to what we had done for the Salt Lake Tabernacle. We also offered new build alternatives, should the decision be made to not reconstruct. Then we waited out several weeks of silence.

I was on vacation June 26, 2011, when I received a phone call from the Presiding Bishopric's office. "The First Presidency is pleased with your report regarding the tabernacle. They have a special request which you must keep strictly confidential and engage the smallest number of your staff as possible. They want you to return and report if the tabernacle remains can be rebuilt into a temple?"

"Absolutely," I said.

I sat for a while at my little bedroom desk, the solid maple table my grandparents used to serve food on to their bed and breakfast cottage guests on the coast of Maine during the 1950s and '60s. I sat and contemplated the assignment. Thoughts flooded my mind as they often did when challenged with a new project.

This time was different, however. I was sitting at my desk dressed as Laurie when I took the phone call. I was unsure if I was committing a sin wearing women's clothing and making myself up this way. I feared I was cutting myself off from the companionship of the Holy Spirit.

I was alone in our house. Marleen had taken our youngest daughter, Tatiana, with her to Rexburg, Idaho, where our oldest son, Bill, was attending school to support his family. Two days before they had welcomed their first child into their student apartment home. I had taken advantage of the empty house, perhaps for the first time during daylight hours, to present as Laurie, part of the effort to find my true self.

Unable to pause the rush of ideas, I went to work and found some drawing paper. In my computer bag was the report we had submitted regarding the tabernacle. It gave me plenty of base drawings to use. The idea of putting the modern temple program into a historic LDS building was familiar to me. Our team had worked on several project ideas for the church's properties in Nauvoo, Illinois, for then-president Gordon B. Hinckley. This had included careful studies of the church's pioneer temples and other historic church buildings.

In subsequent years, as new temple design shifted to historically referenced, classical designs, our particular knowledge of early LDS buildings enabled us to create new designs based on uniquely LDS building forms, such as the temples in Kansas City; Brigham City, Utah; and Philadelphia. It was evident this assignment would be the first opportunity to apply all the knowledge gained to design the modern temple program into an actual historic LDS building.

I envisioned the layout of the rooms located on three floors of the building. Though the tabernacle had a two-story façade, its interior was only ever one level plus a mezzanine balcony. I thought through how the support areas could work, and how patrons would symbolically and physically move through the temple. And I committed to the principle that there would be no visible building additions to the original form of the Tabernacle. Quick sketches were produced describing the three levels of the temple, one excavated below the former main floor, just as we had done at the Salt Lake Tabernacle, plus below grade support spaces beneath the adjacent park, again as existed on Temple Square. Within a short period of time, it was clear and ready to develop. I determined the handful of people I would trust to show these sketches to who would develop the design into a full presentation to the church's leadership.

It was all done while I sat at my grandparents' table presenting as Laurie. I did not understand then, as I do now, the affirming experience it was to create the design of such a special project while being my authentic self. Doing so stripped away decades of guilt and shame regarding my identity and of ever finding true self-expression. I found confidence to move forward with my investigation of my truth. As I sat and designed this new repurposed temple, I was simultaneously redesigning and repurposing myself.

It is difficult to describe how I was changed by this experience. For the next five years as I was compelled to continue to present myself as male, I knew firmly inside I was female, the knowledge I had once possessed as a child and teen but had suppressed for so long. My feelings of anger, anxiety, and frustration were directly related to denial of my true self. Finding and never burying again my gender identity was the key.

Energized by this truth, I increased my study of what I had come to know as transgenderism. I learned I was not alone in feeling gender incongruence and conflict. The proper term for this was gender dysphoria, and it could be mitigated. My eyes were opened as I studied online transgender healthcare issues, the protocols associated with medical transition, and read many stories of social transitions.

It took three months to prepare the full design of the new Provo temple. No more than five or six people outside church leadership were aware of the design's existence when President Thomas S. Monson announced to audible gasps from the congregation in the October 2011 general conference that the Provo Tabernacle would be rebuilt to become the Provo City Center Temple. Then the real work began to develop the design into completed construction plans.

———————

The paradigm shift that occurred at my little table was self-acceptance of my female gender identity that existed in conflict with my physical biology. I now understood this struggle logically. What had not occurred yet for me was a spiritual assurance that would bring peace to the conflict. A month following the announcement of the Provo temple, I was on an overnight flight from Salt Lake City to Lisbon, Portugal. Being unable to sleep on airplanes, I used the time in the dimly lit quiet to journal my thoughts into my smartphone. I documented the case I had made for myself that I was indeed transgender. By the time I arrived in Lisbon, I had something of a personal treatise prepared.

Our team separated and went to our hotel rooms to rest before we began the next several days' efforts of documenting architectural precedent to guide design of the future Lisbon Temple. Once in my room alone, I used the time, as I had frequently done over the past several months, to dress and make myself up as Laurie. I found doing this brought an enormous sense of relief and wholeness of self. I lay on the bed re-reading my treatise, reinforcing to myself, right or wrong, I was truly transgender.

For several months the guilt and shame of such an admission had been eliminated, yet I was still unsure of where God was regarding the issue. Having guided all aspects of my personal and family life, in addition to my ecclesiastical service and project work for the church by means of personal prayer and revelation, I was confident I could learn God's mind concerning me. For the first time ever in my life I knelt, still presenting as Laurie, and prayed, "Dear Heavenly Father, this is me, Laurie Lee, this is who I am …" Despite my confidence, I was unsure of the possible response as I began. "I have studied a lot about what it means to be transgender, and I identify as female ..."

I was amazed by the response I felt—a peaceful assurance and a sensation of joy felt "beyond the veil" that I had finally come to accept myself as Deity always knew me to be, just as I had been created to be. I sat and pondered such an answer for a long while.

The knowledge and assurance that my gender, my eternal spiritual identity was not only acceptable to God, but previously known by God, and mattered enough that there was joy felt in heaven over me catching up to Him cemented my truth! I had, after fifty years, accepted myself as God knew me. The thought brought joy, which penetrated deep within me. Now my real work of change began, but my true identity still lay deep under the rubble of the choices and trappings of my adult lifetime attempting to present as a male, contrary to my nature.

———————

I attended, along with thousands of others, the groundbreaking ceremony for the Provo City Center Temple in May 2012, presided over by Elder Jeffery R. Holland of the church's Quorum of Twelve Apostles. Construction commenced soon thereafter with reinforced concrete applied to permanently strengthen the exterior walls forming a rigid box. This "shell" was then held in place in the air by steel framing while excavation down to forty-five feet below the surface was completed. The form of the tabernacle stood suspended as though it were defying gravity. This was done to accomplish the goal I had from the outset to build no addition to the above-grade historic building. Even the ground we sat on during the groundbreaking would be removed and dressing rooms would be installed beneath our seats.

During the spring and summer of 2012, I started "coming out" as transgender. First to Marleen, then to selected family and close friends, and to our adult children with their spouses. Marleen supported me to dress more androgynously at home away from work. I began meeting with Terri Busch, a trained gender therapist, a true gem of a find in Salt Lake City. Together we strengthened my resolve and excavated deep within me to discover the best path forward for me. Her efforts helped mitigate my gender dysphoria and to cope with the new challenge of familial and social rejection of my truth. At times weekly therapy sessions were all that kept me from crashing to the ground below.

By the summer of 2014 the enormous hole beneath the shell of the temple had been filled with its intended construction: thick footings, the baptistry level, and an intermediate mechanical level. Foundation walls were erected and the shell of the historic building came to rest upon its new supporting structure. At last, detailed work could proceed to make the temple truly beautiful.

August 24, 2014, was the day that I, with informed consent and upon recommendation of my therapist, received my first scripts for hormone replacement therapy; two testosterone blockers, and estradiol. Marleen had been adamant against my starting hormones. But I was convinced this next step was essential and I "could not-not do it any longer." Within a matter of weeks, Marleen surprised me by saying, "I have talked with some of the other wives whose husbands have been struggling with their gender, and I told them what a difference being on hormones has been for you. That you are so much calmer now, less angry and frustrated. I told them they needed to stop waiting and get their husbands on hormones too!"

With the medications, I felt grounded in a way I never had before. My gender dysphoria, including secondary effects of depression, anxiety, and panic disorder, was markedly swept away. I came to appreciate that our bodies and brains rely upon the stimulus of certain hormones to function, and our cells are predisposed with receptors that have sensitivity to one hormone or another. Getting one's hormones finally right is like having run a diesel engine on regular gas for decades before supplying it with the correct diesel fuel. The engine would not survive the wrong fuel for fifty-three years, as I had done. Once again, I found the next level of change and peace I had imagined might be possible while I lay in my hospital bed.

———

The Provo City Center Temple became the 150th temple of the church when it was dedicated for its sacred purposes in March 2016. I was not able to attend the dedication ceremonies with my family.

The following month I risked my employment and came out to my colleagues at work. Then, from the fast-meeting pulpit, I explained to my ward I was transgender and asked for their patience and support towards me and my family as I socially transitioned.

Finally, I asked the leaders of my department at work for accommodation to retain my employment through the process of my social transition. My request was not granted. I was forced to retire from church employment after twenty years of service. The next day I began my new and more beautifully purposed life, living full-time and authentically as Laurie Lee Hall.

In time I began volunteering at Encircle House in Provo, facilitating their Becoming discussions for transgender persons and their family members. One idyllic spring evening, about a year after the temple was dedicated, I stood in the main sitting room of Encircle, alone before the meeting. I gazed out the window at the temple grounds with its gazebo marriage party waiting area, in a lovely park setting, the restored temple façade forming the background. The building, though destroyed by fire, was transformed from a beloved historic tabernacle into a modern temple, serene in its new role of offering the church's highest ordinances on earth.

I stepped towards the window and into the sunlight that streamed in illuminating me, causing my reflection to appear in the window. I beheld my authentic self in service to my LGBTQ siblings. Reflected back was a gracious woman, whole, transformed, and fulfilling the measure of my own creation. My heart swelled with love and gratitude, and I caught tears running down my cheeks.

HAUNTED

JIM CARLSTON (NÉE KATHY CARLSTON)

The Ketamine clinic was full of life on the morning of my first treatment. The office was decorated for Christmas, which was just days away. Familiar faces peeked out from behind the check-in counter. I smiled and waved hello.

"Hey! It's so good to see you! Your nurse is ready for you. You'll be in room 2 today."

I'd been going to this clinic for a year and a half. Once a week, I'd have treatments like vitamin infusions, pain point injections, nutrition consults, and meetings with my doctor. I had been diagnosed with Lyme disease, among other things that my doctor and I were trying to combat.

Today, though, was different. Today was going to be my first course of intravenous ketamine.

It had been a tremendously difficult year. My wife had died by suicide earlier in the summer. My mom had been diagnosed with cancer and was currently on hospice in my aunt's home. My heart was in tatters and I was looking for help and support through the turbulence.

"Alright," my nurse said, "this is going to sting a bit."

The IV flashed, and my nurse hooked the line to the bag. Soon, my eyes were half closed and I was deep under, in a space between.

First, I looked down and I was my mother, resting in her hospice bed, waiting to die from the cancer ravaging her abdomen.

Then, I was my deceased dad as a child, being pushed to the ground on the playground, feeling completely powerless to stop it.

After, I was my late wife, seated on our bed. My body was racked with exhaustion from yet another bout of insomnia and withdrawals from stopping Klonopin. I'd cried all morning, and as I sat there, I'd just formulated my plan to end my life.

I experienced dozens of other mind-bending scenarios from viewpoints of different individuals in my life in my session. It was incredibly intense and felt deeply serious and somber.

But about four-fifths of the way through my trip I saw my wife. She was surrounded by other loved ones who had passed away. They surrounded me and to my horror, started beckoning me to join them in the afterlife.

I had no desire to die, so I resisted their beckoning. The rest of the trip became considerably dark, and finally ended with me pawing off my headphones as the nurse came in because I was back at Columbine, hearing gunshots and sirens.

A few months later I decided to quit my job. I had enough money saved and I felt comfortable working on getting my non-profit off the ground. But soon after leaving my employment, I was bombarded by a series of difficult experiences. Among them, my church amended a harmful policy regarding queer people that had deeply hurt my wife and me, but did so without any apology or acknowledgement of the pain caused, the lives ruined, including my late wife's. I tried my best to cope with these unexpected stresses. But they compounded with my grief over my wife and now deceased mother. I fell into a deep depression, deeper than I have ever previously experienced.

I felt like I was marooned on a sailboat, waiting for days on end for the wind to return. I spent the entire summer waiting, day after day, week after week, month after month. I did what I knew to do about my depression. I worked with my doctor on medication changes, I attempted to eat well and exercise, I diligently went to therapy, but nothing I tried touched it.

My mind started to examine my life, searching and searching for something that felt at all meaningful. I groped for a compelling reason to continue drudging through my pain. In the years previous, my non-profit had always been my answer. But the basic thesis of my non-profit was to try to help fellow shooting survivors see that though things are hard, life is still beautiful and worth living. Unfortunately, in the wake of so much loss, I found that I no longer fully believed this claim.

Still, though, I continued to search for meaning. In July I tried further rounds of ketamine treatment. Luckily, I only had positive ketamine trips with those rounds, and I found that the physical symptoms of my depression lifted almost immediately. I could get out of bed, run errands, and see friends and it wasn't an ordeal to me. However, I continued to be unable to identify a single meaningful goal to pursue.

In early August, I started feeling a tugging at my heart. I remembered the sensation of my wife and my other deceased loved ones beckoning me. This feeling became more and more frequent until it was nearly constant.

I missed my wife and longed to be in her company again. I still could not identify a single reason to continue fighting. So I made a plan and set a date to take my life, about a month away. For a couple of weeks, I felt a sense of profound peace.

"Hey, I picked up some dinner for us. Are you hungry?"

My housemate Jenica was a consistent support through this period. I had not shared my plans to die with her, but she had listened to hours of my processing and grief with kindness and empathy.

"How's this afternoon been for you, friend?"

"Honestly I haven't done much today except watch *Inception* and lay on the couch. I love that movie but it kind of takes me back to the first ketamine trip."

"Howso?"

"Mal spends most of the movie beckoning Dom to join her. It's just not clear if she's permanently dead or if she's just waiting for him to wake up on the next level."

"Hmm. Ya, that makes sense. You know, I've been thinking—what evidence do you have that it was Berta who was the one beckoning you in your trip? It could have been any number of things, neurons firing off in a new way, a subconscious reaction to your grief, a longing to connect back with her out of this loneliness ... and it's far-fetched but I can't rule out some sort of destructive force outside of you trying to have influence."

Our dinner continued and I contemplated Jenica's thoughts for the rest of the night. The next day, I called for help. Friends and family surrounded me as I checked myself into LDS Hospital's psych ward. I didn't know much, but I knew I was safe. Safe to share the extent of what had been on my mind, and physically safe from myself. Between my hospital psych hitting a home run with my meds and the relief of finally being able to be candid, I began to get better.

As I was preparing to be released, I still couldn't identify a meaningful goal, but I felt a deep sense of hope that I could continue to search for it because of the love I felt from my community.

My cousin Rebecca picked me up. Rebecca was one of the last remnants of my tattered family that I felt I could be comfortable with. The plan was for me to stay with my late wife's family in Mapleton. Rebecca's car and we started our journey, drove through the Avenues and stopped at the light at 400 South and 700 East.

"Rob's planning to fly out to see you on the 20th. Does that work for you?"

"Ya, I think that'd work."

I'd always loved Rebecca's brother, Rob, and smiled at the thought of being able to see him. Rebecca paused for a moment, seeming to mull a thought over.

"So ... Is this your way of asserting power?"

I stared at her, dumbfounded. Several moments passed.

She backpedaled and said, "I can tell I just stepped in some shit. Can you explain to me why what I said was hurtful?"

"Well, when I hear that, it seems like a way of saying that I went to the hospital for attention. That I'm faking to be manipulative. But anyone taking a look at my life for more than two seconds would have some understanding of why I would want to give up. My wife's gone, my parents are dead, so much else is wrong with the world and I just feel so hollow inside."

"Hmm. That makes sense. Thank you for explaining. So anyway ..."

We drove on and finally made it to the Marquez's. Berta's mom, Rebecca, and I talked 'til late in the night. In the conversation Rebecca asked me to sign over my power of attorney to one of them, but luckily didn't have the form with her.

Rob called the next day. I told him about my sadness, how I wasn't sure how to fix it.

"It's like I tell my seminary students. You need to surrender to Jesus."

I sat in silence.

"I really think He can fix your same-sex attraction."

I winced at the term that had harmed so many people I loved.

"You would be so much happier if you would just be straight," he explained. "You just need to pray to him."

As I sat on my bed, it took a moment to realize that my jaw hung open. Feelings of a stunned disappointment washed over me. I had known that Rob and I had different opinions on queerness, but I had no idea how antiquated his beliefs about me were.

"Rob, I did reparative therapy for eight years, including the time I was at BYU," I reminded him, inwardly begging him to see me. "I prayed every night. I've cried so many tears over this. I can assure you that if anyone was to be able to change their orientation it would have been me. I'm really triggered by religious talk; can we please talk about something else?"

"I just really think you didn't try hard enough. In Corinthians, it says—"

I raised my voice.

"Rob, really, I need to talk about something else."

"Look Kathy. It's easy. Just ask Jesus to heal you."

"I really can't do this. I need to go."

I finally hung up the phone and sobbed into my pillow.

Over the next couple of days, I had many profound therapy appointments through Flourish Therapy, beautiful get togethers with friends, and delicious dinners with my in-laws. I found myself feeling more and more stable, even though I still experienced that same empty feeling at the end of the day, and even through the anger and sadness I felt over my loved ones' words.

After I had spent a few weeks recuperating, I received some deeply distressing news.

I had asked Rob to reschedule his trip so that I could focus on my healing. He decided to make the trip anyway. I felt that the best decision for me was to keep my distance so I refused to see him.

I learned from friends who had talked to Rebecca that Rob had made the trip because he believed that I was not going to survive this period. He believed that I was going to imminently die and went against my wishes so that he would have a chance to say his final goodbyes.

When I heard this, it felt like a gut punch. The more I thought about it, the more I boiled over with anger at the profound disrespect and lack of faith shown to me.

Ultimately, I felt that my situation and my heart were deeply misunderstood. From my perspective, my asking for help and admitting myself should not be interpreted as a giving up. It was not an invitation to have my family plan my funeral. My going to the hospital was a sign that I was fighting to get better. I needed support in that recovery, not their presumptive goodbyes.

As I processed my feelings of anger, I had an epiphany. Living, even if only to prove them wrong about me, became enormously appealing. Continuing on with my life out of a sense of pure, unadulterated spite had never been a valid option that I had considered. I'd heard of the concept, but it hadn't resonated with me until that moment. But why not prove them wrong?

The following thought kept coming back to me over the next few days: Why should I settle to only haunt those who don't believe in me from the grave when I can haunt them from the flesh by living a full, beautiful life?

Despair was what everyone expected.

What if I lived a life of joy instead?

Why not go get it? Why not find another wonderful partner and grow old by her side? Why not work together to help tons of people with her?

Why not build and develop into a position of financial wellness and help others do the same?

Why not cultivate the garden of relationships with those in my life who *get* me, who *see* me and enjoy my company? Who not only "love" me but show me time and time again that they *like* me and delight in my well-being? Why not grow that garden of friendships and roll around in the beauty of them like freshly cut grass?

"Jenica, it's like this metric ton of a burden has been lifted from my shoulders. I feel a physical sense of relief. I feel excited about the future. It's like I've found an end of the unending road I'd felt trapped on. I finally have meaningful goals to work toward. It's like a volcano erupted in my soul. Out of that eruption flowed goals that seemed unequivocally worth fighting for."

"Shit, Kathy." I heard her voice through the phone. "I am so grateful this has finally happened for you. You've worked so hard toward healing. I can't wait to see what you do."

Four years later, I have found other beautiful reasons to keep living. I've started accomplishing the goals that resonated so deeply back then. I've gotten to a financially better place, and each day I delight in my garden of friends and loved ones.

And I still feel a profound desire to get out there and do some haunting.

A HIDDEN LOVE STORY

GERADO SUMANO

The winter semester of my sophomore year at BYU-Idaho became the stage of a queer love story that defied all odds.

Growing up in Yucatán, Mexico, one of the most conservative places in the country, my childhood was steeped in the teachings of my devout Mormon parents who strongly believed on the importance of eternal families and marriage between a man and a woman.

It was a Sunday after church when my parents called me into their room. "Why hadn't you told us you had a problem with same-sex attraction?" my dad asked.

A heavy silence enveloped the room. Anxiety flooded my thoughts, thinking about worst-case scenarios, including the fear of being cast out of my home for having feelings I never chose. The secrecy surrounding my "same-sex attraction" had been my silent burden for as long as I could remember.

Tears streamed down my mom's face as she implored, "We can find you help. You can overcome this."

"God has a plan for you and through the atonement you will be able to change," echoed my dad.

Feeling the weight of their expectations, without hesitation I said, "I am willing to try. I want to go on a mission and I know I have to fix this." It was hard to look at either of them. I couldn't bear to see their disappointment in me.

My mom tearfully suggested, "We've found a therapist who has been able to overcome these attractions himself and he helps other men like you. It's called conversion therapy. If you have a sincere desire to change, you can overcome this, Gerardo."

I just needed that strong desire to change and everything was going to be fine.

By the end of my mission, I had convinced myself that upon returning, I would marry a woman and lead a life in perfect alignment with the covenant path. However, when I got home, reality hit me with a force I couldn't have anticipated. My attractions towards men remained, the conversion therapy hadn't worked, and my unwavering commitment to serving the best mission I possibly could did not bring about the miracle I sought. It didn't take long before my belief in a life that conformed to my faith's expectations began to crumble. The disparity between my true self and the path I had set upon became undeniable. It was the beginning of a profound internal transformation, as I realized that my true happiness would lay in embracing the authenticity of who I was rather than continuing to hide behind a facade of conformity.

I decided to go to BYU-Idaho.

My decision, particularly as a gay Mormon who had just come to terms with an inability to fully adhere to the church's teachings, is a complex one. Several factors influenced it. Notably, the prevailing cultural norm in Mexico is that young adults reside with their parents until marriage. Therefore, opting for BYU-Idaho presented an escape from this cultural convention while also offering my parents a sense of reassurance. This institution, closely aligned with the most rigorous tenets of Mormon beliefs, provided them with a comforting assurance that I was in an environment supportive of our faith's principles, thus putting their minds at ease.

Once at BYU-Idaho, life was on the upswing, but a lingering sense of loneliness persisted. Surrounded by a marriage-centric culture, where my heterosexual peers constantly embarked on dates and nurtured serious relationships that led to marriage, my yearning for a meaningful relationship grew stronger. It was challenging to be in a place where even if I found someone to share a beautiful connection, it would have to remain concealed.

Then, I met Zach.

Our story kicked off with a simple swipe on a dating app, and from there, we arranged the most straightforward of dates: Wendy's followed by a movie. Zach, with his infectious smile and a 2001 Toyota Camry, arrived to pick me up. Dressed in the cutest button-up shirt, he radiated genuine interest in discovering more about me and my hobbies, "So do you use LightBox for your photography?" he asked.

Attempting to be polite, I responded with a smile, "Oh yes," though, truth be told, I had never heard about such a thing.

At Wendy's, we both settled on the four-for-four deal. Awkwardly, I initiated conversation, "So you like four for fours?"

Zach sweetly replied, "Yes! It's the best bang for your buck!"

Seated at a table, I couldn't help but admire his beauty. He was tall—6'1"—and had brown eyes and an adorable smile. Sneaking a moment when I thought he was not watching, I texted my one friend who knew about my date with Zach, gushing, "Omg! He is super cute!"

Our dialogue took an unexpected turn from hobbies to personal revelations. Zach asked, "So, do your parents know about you?"

Laughing, I responded, "They know about my 'same-sex attraction,' and they are expecting me to marry a woman. They don't know I'm on a date with a man. What about you?"

Zach shared, "Ironically, I chose BYU-Idaho to escape the restrictions at home. My parents want me to stay faithful in the church and avoid dating men. It's too much pressure, and I can't be who they want me to be. Their overbearingness was getting frustrating, so here I am." Our stories and reasons for coming to BYU-Idaho bore a striking resemblance.

As we walked to the movie theater my desire to hold his hand clashed with my fear of someone seeing or recognizing us. Rexburg is a college town filled with LDS students and professors. We could be expelled if someone told on us.

As we entered the theater and the movie started, I looked around and was surprised that we were the only ones there. Nervously, I commented, "I guess the movie must not be very popular."

Zach, with a smile, responded, "I guess we chose the perfect movie then," as he reached out to softly hold my hand. My heart raced as the movie began, and we gradually moved closer and closer. Turning to him, I couldn't resist a kiss. I was over the moon. He was undeniably the best kisser.

From that moment on, not a single day passed without us being inseparable.

My beautiful relationship with Zach flourished in the shadows, hidden from the watchful eyes of a community that could neither comprehend nor accept our love. We were unable to openly share our relationship, burdened by the fear of exposure and the potential consequences. The ever-present fear of being reported to the school and the potentially life-altering ramifications loomed over us, particularly for me as an international student. The risk of being sent back to Mexico, a place that felt increasingly distant from the life I was building, was a reality we couldn't ignore.

We got to know each others' families. Zach's family lived just thirty minutes from Rexburg, and I visited their home, though our true relationship remained concealed. Zach also joined me on a visit to Mexico, where he proposed to me during the enchanting Isla Mujeres sunset. During his visit, he met my parents, although he was introduced to them as nothing more than a friend. It pained me that we couldn't reveal our engagement at that time, yet we held onto the hope that one day, we would unveil our happiness and openly share our love without the need to conceal it.

As graduation day arrived, it marked the culmination of our secret love story, opening the door to a new chapter in our lives. We emerged from the shadows, unburdened by secrecy and fear, ready to embark on our shared journey. Undeniably, the road to acceptance within our families was a gradual one, marked by its own set of trials. Rebuilding fractured family relationships has taken time, patience, and a concerted effort, yet Zach and I stand united through every hardship, finding solace in each other's loving support.

In the soft morning light of our lazy Sundays, Zach and I usually kickstart the day in our chill kitchen, surrounded by the comforting smells of his coffee and freshly made pancakes. We sit down at the table, our fingers naturally finding each. Between bites, our chatter usually flows around the easy rhythm of our shared life. Our trio of dogs, forever on snack patrol, eyeball us for any potential treats. It is a simple, feel-good routine, a snapshot of the life we've built together. The way our love smoothly fits into the everyday stuff, from sneaky glances to inside jokes, speaks volumes. Around that table, just the two of us and our four-legged crew, we soak up the pure joy in the laid-back magic of our suburban groove. Every one of those mornings feels like a reminder of the beautiful but crazy love story we're living. It's a love that's blossomed in the face of tough times, rising above all the challenges that once kept us hidden.

COLOUR ME QUEER, OR, ELECTRIC BLUE

KEL PURCILL

My first taste of queer potential was electric blue. Tingling, brain-swamping, guttural deep tones of vibrant blue with impossible black glimmers. Slick tiles under a constant indigo light, grout lines dark and contrary to the curves and gasps of the silver-edged bodies tangled against the wall, against each other. Against my understanding of possibility.

Electric blue. Two people kissing. Two men.

Men. Kissing.

Men kissing each other.

Electric blue and beautiful and maybe the local power station had exploded because a thrum of *this* and *then that means* and *why didn't anyone say?* and neon fizz diving so far into my bones I had to stand up, stagger, sit, stand again. To pour my wonder and joy into a laugh I caught in my hands, not seeing the TV screen but my entire future floating in vibrant, feral, electric blue.

A joy I then choked on. What hope has a fifteen-year-old redhead in nowhere, New South Wales, got of not marrying a guy? Until then all I'd dared hope for was a bloke who wouldn't mind my books. What other potential was there? None. No alternatives, no suggestions of something else available, just like there was only the one road leading out from my tiny town, one high school to attend, one future I was already fighting.

Electric blue. The potential of it—years before I knew the word queer—was hopeful and appalling, as tangled and stunning, as baffling and incandescent as that one scene caught accidentally, serendipitously, tragic and precious. A flash of blue, broadcast close to midnight and somehow seen in a tiny pocket of rural Australia, deep in the shadowed mountains and stubborn, rural culture of the early '90s.

The Australian Bowerbird collects and displays tokens and small precious finds as part of its mating ritual. Satin bowerbirds were in the wild country and farms around the towns I grew up, always in the mountain gullies and thick bush, the males darkly feathered, the females dull greens, all generally unremarkable. They're not tiny, not huge, not delicate, not outrageously feathered or even melodious. They're just … bowerbirds. Doing bowerbird things.

I hadn't always lived in that town. My family had moved around for work, following the sweat-crusted collar of my dad around the country. He was temperamental, demanding, inconsistent, and huge, a constant storm throwing our orbits into silence, into distant corners, into a cosmic cloud of *this is what a man is, does, and does and don't you dare think otherwise.* There was only black and white in his world, in our home, and white was supreme. Flashes of fury, of the clay bruised belt slicing out of pant loops, all lightning hot and blinding grey-white, vicious, fading to invisible, never spoken of, sly fanged after-images conveyed in a look. He was a linesman, feeding power lines from the hydro-electric stations to the country, manipulating his power through our lives. That grey-white fury swallowed all color, gorged on fear, spilled binary fury/not fury into everything, even with eyes scrunched tight.

My science homework said light contains all colors, even though it looks so bright. Not the grimy white I lived in. There was no space for my electric blue there, no sleek black glimmers or silver curves.

I pushed the electric blue down. Deep down, beneath the wind ruffled surface of family drama and history, below the immoveable decrees of can and cannots of "in this town" and "in this family" we do and do nots. Pushed it down, and sideways, carving out a silver-edged cavern of sparkles and maybes, secrets and longing. Too precious to visit. Guarded. Avoided. Dreamed of, hotly imagined, hidden deeper. Crystalline veins of impossible black. Electric blues.

When seeking a mate, male bowerbirds will prepare a bower, bending calf-high grasses and twigs in a u-shape, wide enough for a bowerbird to hop along without touching the sides, about as long as your forearm and curving in at the ends and top. Bowerbirds organize trinkets, stones, flowers, shells, any found treasure to best focus attention on the bower, with an eye to detail, scale and perspective in every placement, every readjustment, the chosen approach to the bower. It is a study in deliberate contrast, with nothing to distract the eye. The intent is connection, interest, focus: there is dirt, there is the bower, and in-between? Intention. Art. Wonder.

My second taste of queer potential was fuzzy brown. The brown of my best friend's cheeks, familiar, warm and not seen in person in a few years, living in different towns on different sides and vertebrae of the continent's mountain range. We slammed together, delirious at being together again, laughing and shouting then

flailing

apart as we realized hormones and body changes had definitely happened in our absence, neon signs and goose bumps stuttering our tongues, twitching our past comfort and ease into something … else. We split off, away, and apart; Monty to swim and wrestle with his cousins, me to curl up reading in the lounge room, our faces smooshed by each other's families as boozy adults teased, admonished, and observed variations of "look how much you've grown!" Separate, still watching each other at a cautious distance. We pulled back together within hours, our friendship since childhood and recent, shared, posted letters demanding better, more immediate contact and connection—and we talked. He showed off his growing moustache, rolled his eyes but let me touch it, snapping his teeth when I came close enough and snort laughing when I punched him. He growled in person about the jerks bullying me at school, his latest basketball game. I explained, in detail, the plot of *The Hobbit*. All of it was warm brown, traced with the black of his eyelashes, the dark odd shape in his dark brown left eye, the flavored milk we shared between us as we talked music and high school and nothing at all. Everything was a warm brown, the brown of his cheeks, the cozy heat of connection like the firewood's potential I'd stacked at home, the whorl of tree rings our own personal orbits of being seen exactly where we were.

Someone eventually yelled for everyone to come in for dinner, people streaming out of the dusk into the kitchen, cigarette smoke curling against the florescent light. A stream of people going in, my sister, a cousin, Monty, someone else, then me—only to smack face first into mixed cheering and groaning, adults elbowing each other, Monty's older brother, on leave from the Navy for the weekend, looking at me weirdly, my dad with his hand out, Monty's dad putting cash into it.

They'd been betting on if I'd be right after Monty, or him after me, a surety that being teenagers and hormones would have us stupid—and fair game for bets. Monty's cheeks were flushed, mortified, though he tried to play it off as nothing, a new brown that was somehow both breathlessly adjacent and distant from the warmth of before. All my face showed were how much my freckles clashed when I was embarrassed. We kept to different corners of rooms then, sharing the occasional rolled eyes, smirk or tossed tennis ball, trying not to let any of our connection slip away.

His brother kissed me later that night—quick, a light taste of my lips. It was an empty chip packet blown for a moment against sun-warmed tree bark.

Monty avoided me after that weekend.

I survived it.

Mostly.

A tree-stump, hollowed, appeared in the secret cavern, electric blue running gentle ripples across the soft, weary, exposed curving grain. A hiding place of secrets, of safety, of *this is mine*, even if it did leave splinters in my fingertips and impossible futures. None of it was for sale. None of it was for amusement. If anyone saw it, they would break it. I wasn't sure I could survive that.

I sank it deeper.

Straightness was a stale, bore water grey, of mold that spews overnight, of milk split, separated. I tried it. For years. I'd been torn from the mountains to a humid, northern coast, where my family sweated and stank like the cows that look cancerous, ponderous, a mangrove pong and heartache becoming as familiar as the number of days left until … GONE. High school completed, family ignorance and stubbornness brewing, festering, infesting until yet again and (as expected and hard fought against) one road was available, one road to a possible future.

I took it.

I left the town, the coast, a boyfriend, too many family secrets and expectations with two suitcases, secondhand sunglasses and the electric blue all but forgotten in the cool, mountain edged past. I signed up, flew south, collected dog tags, summer whites, a rifle, assorted uniform pieces, a paycheck, and wondered if this itchiness was freedom. I was away, gone, not quite to my mountains, but close enough. Rules to follow, whistles and orders to learn, new customs and boots and culture to squeeze into.

I didn't want to. Not this.

But maybe grey was all that was available.

Bowerbirds will scavenge whatever is available. There's definite selection; some found petals or metal never picked up, some curl of drinking straw or berry never flown back to base. Bowerbirds are absolute kleptomaniacs, taking whatever it is that catches their attention, their imagined design. Used syringes have been found in urban bowers, lying near wrinkled scraps of magazine pages and tiny, scavenged coins; shells and shriveled latex posed near sandal straps and coral in tropical bowers. Everything is fair game for bowerbirds, anything could be used.

The color of desire isn't on a flag, not given in convenient rank and sign. If it was, maybe I wouldn't have been blinded by the white gold of her hair. No fraternization allowed, no sex on base, no allowance for what you want to wear when you go on leave. No male friends, be grey, be not you. Sharp edges, tight buns and crisp, marched turns. All out there. Outside this room, this allotted barrack, this division, this little square of table/bed/wardrobe, this isle where these two naval officers' caps are placed casually, habitually, on the flat, hours from the coast. Those demands are outside from here. Here, where my spine is an ocean's wave. My ears seashells, filled with a sweet tsunami of *this, this, this*, moving against the white gold beach of thigh and tide lines. After, a light careless trace of a finger against my shoulder. A memory swirled, caramelized: the trailing edge of a towel writing nonsense in the dirt. I was bringing the clothes in off the line, back in my mountains, perplexed by the dangling towel. There was no peg missing—not on the line, not on the ground, not on the towel itself. Something about the slow, patient glide of the towel edge snagged my thoughts, calmed them, *hush, this*, and I stood watching, wondering in some light, untethered way what it would be like to be touched or touch like that. In the now she hummed a little and licking my lips I tasted her again. The memory, the light caress, salt and sweat and—

She left. The bed, the room, our friendship, all of it. She'd punished herself somehow, in being with me, some jagged, twisted reason that cut us both. That taste of queer potential was golden blonde, caramelizing at the edges into sandy brown, a meeting of desire and connection, where the harsh burnt summer sand hits the darker, sweeter, sea-licked cool.

The trinkets, their colors and their placement, are what initially attracts potential bowerbird mates—not song, not plumage displays, only the deliberate angle of this pebble, this plastic milk cap, this petal. Each piece is selected by shape, composition, by actual ultra-violet visibility—by reasons unseen by so many others passing by, stumbling in, impatient or ignorant or uncaring as to what treasures lie right there. Each piece ordered, considered, turned just so and deliberately there, and here, and again. Each piece, each chosen and framed to focus the gaze, create an atmosphere for attraction, for a possible future, for connection.

All that is decades ago. I'm comfortably, brilliantly, in my forties. Divorced (from a guy) over a decade ago, tempted to maybe date again (probably not a guy). I'm comfortably in my forties, as luxurious and open as the sunset, expansive, generous, and blatant. There's nothing pushed down anymore, nothing hidden. It's all in where you look, the angle you take that leads you to happiness, to contentment.

Favorite time of day, an app's quiz asks. Sunset. One word answer, to the kaleidoscoping arrival when all the colors merge, swirl, adapt, and flare. That one, stunning moment, where the sky shows the night and universe brush their cheeks together, breathe, and sigh, all deep flares of indigos, blacks, electric and astounding. The colors you adore, wonder the names of, live … choose to be there, deliberate, gorgeous, and blatant.

Each piece encourages the gaze, the possible mate, the potential future, in towards the point of it all. Come, says the bowerbird. This is what I have found. These are all part of my journey to this moment. Come closer, see what I have created for you. Rest. Sit here, let me tell you, surprise you, share with you about myself, my choices, my hopes, every move reflecting who I am here, in this moment, from all that has come before.

The satin bowerbird's treasures are blue.

NOTES FROM THE FIELD
(AN ARCHEOLOGY OF GENDER)

JACLYN FOSTER

Whenever Chris Pine comes up in conversation, I can barely breathe. Breathlessly, I talk, and talk, and talk about him to people, as if I'm begging. "Please, hear what I'm telling you about me." But they don't, of course. How could they? I don't even know what I'm telling them about myself. "I want you to see me exactly as Chris Pine, but not at all as a man?" Even typing this now, I don't know.

If I let my hair grow until it curls around my chin, will you remember its default state is short?

If anything, my urge to babble about Pine seems to function as more of a red herring. "Wait … I thought you were a lesbian?" my classmate frowns. "No, I'm in love with Chris Pine *because* I'm a lesbian," I begin, launching into an extended explanation of the "Chris Pine dresses like a non-binary lesbian" niche TikTok series. Like Cady Heron, I can hear people getting bored with me, but I can't stop. The cardiology professor calls our class to attention, and I trail off, grateful. I open Twitter. Chris Pine has short hair and a grey beard now—the fans are hyping up his new look. I feel an aching sense of loss. I feel faintly ridiculous.

When I was twelve, my mom came home from Old Navy with two pairs of shorts. One grey, one olive green. In my memory, they look like cargo shorts without the puffy pockets. My mom had scoured malls and outlet stores far and wide for "modest" shorts—I was adamantly opposed to short shorts, going so far as to draw a full-sized copy of *For the Strength of Youth* out of my bright yellow purse in the Hollister dressing room, where my mom had tried to convince me to settle for some mid-thigh lime green sweatpant-style lounge-wear. Finally, my mom thought, she had struck gold at Old Navy.

Instead, to both her and my surprise, I burst into sobs. Not the usual emotional tears of a preteen girl, but deep, shuddering, gut-wrenching sobs, coming from a place I didn't know existed. "But *what* don't you like about them?" my mom asked. "Is there anything in particular? Could you maybe make them work with a different shirt?"

I couldn't explain it. She returned the shorts.

"Sorry, this smells a little bit like cologne, is that all right?" my barber asked, sounding concerned.

"Oh yeah, sure, no worries," I replied nonchalantly. She worked the product into my hair. This was my third haircut with her, and the best so far. My horrendous luck with short haircuts had turned into a bit of a joke—the lesbian cursed with hair that defied clippers. Something about giving birth to my son had changed its texture to a mirror image of my dad's. ("They keep trying to blend it and saying, oh no, there's a line, right? And then they keep clipping and clipping?" he commiserated.) I had grown my hair out for eight months after my first haircut with this barber, then at the return appointment, brought a careful selection of photos. Cameron Esposito, a young man who looked like an extra on a '90s television show, a person turned to the side so you couldn't see their face well enough to gender them either way.

Most people wouldn't have returned for a second appointment, but this barber was the first I'd found who was willing to accidentally cut my hair *too* short, instead of giving me what turned into a bob within a week. My trust had paid off, the second haircut had gone fine, so I returned for a third, this time only bringing the young man's picture, dropping the carefully curated gender spectrum. "It's sort of like, uh, Dean from *Gilmore Girls*?" I offered. My barber's eyes lit up. "Oh, I love *Gilmore Girls*! Don't you think Missoula is like Star's Hollow?" The ensuing conversation stretched my hazy memories of watching *A Year in the Life* during 3:00 a.m. breastfeeding sessions to their limits, but at the end, I had the best short haircut I'd ever had. I watched myself in the mirror as she worked the cologne-scented product into the roots, suddenly seized with a conviction that I needed to smell this intoxicating all the time.

I love this product! Where did you get it? I almost ask. The words die on my lips. I remember that smelling like this is an inconvenience, something I need an apology for. I tip 30 percent. I hurry out to my car.

But the idea of smelling like that again won't leave my mind, like the stray hair in your mouth you can't seem to fish out. One day at Target, I venture into the men's grooming section. Sweat trickles down the back of my calf despite the aggressive air conditioning, and I try to select a scent while a black KN94 covers my face, obscuring my jawline (weak even for a woman's). This is impossible. It doesn't help that all the products scream "FOR MEN" in large, reassuring letters—I picture them like an incongruous beacon on my bathroom counter at home.

Whenever I do find a product I like, I'm sure I will be almost annoyingly blasé about it. Someone will catch a whiff on a sweaty summer's day, or my mom will notice when she comes for a visit. "Is that … men's deodorant?" they'll ask, and I'll reply with a condescending eye roll, "Isn't it silly that we gender *scents*?" "It is very silly," they will agree—I can be exhausting to argue with. But their agreement will irritate me too. I need a devil's advocate for my gender.

"Can you believe the women's product is $6.99 and this is $3.99? Imagine paying almost twice as much because we've decided 'burnt amber' is carried on the Y chromosome," I'll steamroll on. And they'll agree, of course, that my enlightened view of sex and gender has met my pioneer thriftiness (in a spectacularly casual manner). The scene plays in my mind as I finally hurry away from the men's aisle, the sweat now trickling down my back and pooling under my armpits. The scent of Secret Powder Fresh wafts up through my fit-tested mask.

———

"I just like winter so much better," I complained to a classmate from small-town Montana. "I don't know how to dress in the summer. I need layers!"

"Oh right, because you have all your uhhh flannels and stuff," my classmate said. I blinked. We'd known each other for three weeks, none of them colder than a high of 85°.

"Right," I replied.

A few months later, I realize I am wearing a flannel shirt under a flannel jacket. "Slowly removing my flannel to reveal a second, smaller flannel underneath," I tweet. *How did he know?* I wonder.

When I was a child, I loved bowling shoes. I fantasized about stealing the gaudy, uncomfortable shoes from the alley, fuzzy failing Velcro and slippery soles worth suffering for in the Calgary winter. In retrospect, I think I wanted leather wingtips, or the type of wardrobe where I might conceivably pair an outfit with playful men's dress shoes.

I didn't realize that's what I wanted, though. As a child, *butch* wasn't a gender expression I had heard of—the two options were "tomboy" (basketball shorts, actual basketball) and "normal" (femme). I had horrible hand-eye coordination: therefore, femme. I studied femininity like it was an extra credit class, practiced it like an instrument. *I'm going to get a good grade in femme, something that is both normal to want and possible to achieve*, jokes the snarky, self-assured version of myself that exists only when I get to retell my stories. In reality, though, I was just twelve and lonely, and wanted to be good. I wanted so badly to be good.

When my sister got married, I planned my outfit meticulously. A trendy silhouette, that I might wear in the broader non-Mormon world, but from DownEast Basic, appropriate for standing demurely outside the temple (COVID regulations rendering the question of my non-entry slightly moot). A neutral palette but saturated enough to avoid washing me out. Layers adaptable to the vagaries of Calgary in May. Heels I could stand in for hours. Softly curled hair. Makeup that my sister approvingly pronounced "very good—but nobody does that much eyeshadow anymore." The only ding on my A- final exam in Femme.

And it *was* a final exam. I had spent the pandemic watching my wife discover femininity, the joy and euphoria radiating from her in ways they never had for me. I don't like this outfit, I realized as I tried to document it in my selfies. I like that everyone *else* will like this outfit. When my brother-in-law got married the next February, I wore a suit.

A few years ago, I floated the idea to a few friends that I might be non-binary. They were immediately supportive. "Jaclyn is so *handsome!*" "Yasss, my liege!" Ugh, never mind.

My sister bombarded me with outfit inspo for the Taylor Swift Eras concert. "Does she know I'm in my 50s," my mom complained, scrolling with me through pages and pages of nightclub outfits. That afternoon, I went to Goodwill and found a rainbow sequin mini skirt. I had never worn a skirt that short. Over the months, an outfit came together—snake patterned fishnet tights, the bandeau mini skirt, a black crop top, a black choker, a red lip. Distinctly femme, but not a flavor I'd ever tried before. As I did my makeup in my sister-in-law's living room, shower mirror suction cupped to a window, I had the fleeting sense that I was participating in some form of drag. I chuckled to myself, diligently blending and tracing. Like riding a bike.

"Something smells good," my sister-in-law remarked. "*You* smell good."

"Oh uh, I might have used Isaiah's stuff in the shower. Also his cologne. Sorry if that's weird, I needed to balance out the outfit." Sydney rolled her eyes a little and laughed. I had arrived last night in a muscle tank and 5' gym shorts, and before the evening was through, I had insisted on making a quick trip to Home Depot to install their pantry shelves. ("Wanna see a dyke tweet," my friend had jokingly quoted when I live-tweeted the process.)

And now I was wearing, I realized, what was essentially a very enjoyable costume. With every step closer to Lumen Field, the crowd became more concentrated with superbly happy women. We all looked each other up and down, beaming, thrilled. I noted the butches, the mascs, and the men in the crowd. *I'd wear that shirt. I'd also wear that shirt. Oh, I NEED to find a shirt like that.* But I found I didn't regret my femme-flavored Reputation outfit, either. It was a special occasion.

We filed into the stadium, watching behind-the-scenes commentary on music videos I'd failed to bone up on. ("This concert has too much homework," I had complained to my coworker. "When I saw Muse, there wasn't ANY homework.") One video in particular confused me. "What is Jake Gyllenhaal doing in this video?" I asked my wife. She looked at me strangely. The scene cut away to Taylor in the makeup chair, becoming a man. Taylor discussing the process of employing a movement coach, Taylor cracking up laughing the first time she tried to adjust her crotch while manspreading.

I grinned. "This is great. There is truly no other way I would choose to be introduced to this one." Later, my wife and I scream-sung "The Man" at each other, both effulgent for completely different reasons.

I bought an "any pronouns" pin to wear on my white coat at the pharmacy. Well, I actually bought three "any pronouns" pins—they each had different genders, and it was too difficult to decide which I liked best. (Once they arrived, I realized the "barbed wire heart" was probably too edgy for work, and the art deco pin had a white background that would fade into the coat, leaving the green enamel leaf as the designated Undefined Work Gender).

I added it quietly, under my "I love vaccines" syringe and opposite my "you are safe with me" Pride flag. I found I didn't feel nervous, or even expectant. I was just curious. Would anyone notice? Would they say anything? What would they say? It would almost be funnier if they didn't. Every day that passed without comment, my amusement deepened.

One morning, I opened the pharmacy with our manager. The first hour at the pharmacy is always quiet, and after filling a few prescriptions, she turned to me. "The other day, I said 'thank you ma'am'," she began nonchalantly, "And I'm worried I might have misgendered you." She didn't sound particularly worried, which was how I liked it. Clearly, she'd had versions of this conversation before.

"It is actually incredibly difficult to misgender me," I chuckled. "I just want people to use whatever rolls off the tongue, but I don't really care *what* rolls off the tongue. I don't like it when adults call me 'mama' at my kids' appointments, and I don't like it when gay men call me 'girlfriend.'" She nodded, and I returned to counting pills by fives.

Later, I showed my coworker photos of the Taylor Swift concert, then for good measure, old photos of the Muse concert. "It was during my goth phase," I noted, smiling at my black lipstick and fake orbital piercing.

"Your hair was so *long!*" she exclaimed, sounding genuinely surprised. As though she'd never imagined me wearing anything but my thrifted men's chinos and button-down Hawaiian shirts. As though its default state had always been short.

———

No matter how long the list of check-boxed genders stretches on an online survey form, I want to scroll down to the bottom and click "other." But then the little box pops up—"(explain) _____."

Explain?

My gender is like the double slit experiment. It changes based on whether you are observing it, and any explanation I give will immediately become incorrect upon you reading it.

This feels like gender homework, and I am playing gender hooky.

I am non-binary in a statistical sense but not in the sense of a coherent, androgynous individualized gender identity, which is how you'll most likely read that particular checked box.

My gender is whatever Chris Pine had going on at the 2023 Cannes Film Festival.

Most people's genders are diastereomers, cis and trans, but mine is an enantiomer. I'm actually terrible at recognizing chiral centers, but sometimes the light shines through at an odd angle.

My gender is whatever answer is funniest in the moment.

I identify as Heisenberg's uncertainty gender. By filling out this box and collapsing the wave function, I may know the speed of the gender, but I can no longer tell you its location.

None gender, left lesbian.

My gender is non-Newtonian. Under non-stressful conditions it behaves as a fluid, but under rigid, stressful conditions (society) it acts like a solid. No, not "genderfluid," it's the same gender the entire time.

I would very much like to be excluded from this narrative, one that I have never asked to be a part of.

Have you read *The Technology of Gender?* The author posits gender as a web of social connections, with individuals as the nodes. Thus, gender is both produced *by* society and produced *within* the individual—and these two processes of co-production are inextricable from one [character limit exceeded].

My pronouns are "I" and "me"—the rest of this sounds like a you problem.

Explain.

If the form is going to be analyzed in aggregate, I scroll back up and check "non-binary," like a little confessional booth embedded in Qualtrics. If it's going to be read by an authority figure, I check "woman." Sometimes I decide it's worth it to risk answering the form with one of the many "not quite wrong" boxes, to plant my inconvenient flag and deal with a well-intentioned hassle.

The best, though, is when they forget to make it a required question, and I leave it blank.

YOU AND ME:
SO HAPPY TOGETHER

MONICA DELGADO

You and I have a complicated history. After half a century on the planet together, we're just starting to be comfortable with each other. I know that's on me and not you. It's hard knowing that. I try not to carry the burden too heavily as I'm softening to the idea that the barriers between us are not my fault. They were determined long before you and I ever met, fueled by history, social institutions, and cultural constructs. It's still rough knowing I went along with it for so long though. I thought it was right. I thought I was happy.

You were a gift from God, a loan to be called back one day with the expectation of being returned in the same pristine condition in which you arrived. You were to be meticulously cared for, kept clean (as they told me what clean meant), and not so much as dishonorably soiled, or otherwise face dire eternal consequences. You were also to be a present to my husband on our wedding night. Your purity, valued the same as gold and rubies, was the ultimate offering. And then, you were to be the holy vessel that carried children. My greatest aspiration was to be used up in the service and glory of God. And, if I did everything right, there would be nothing left of you for me, and in that I would fulfill the measure of my creation. I embodied these teachings and I thought I was happy.

As a result, I didn't inhabit you.

I didn't want to live in all of you anyway. Somehow, I absorbed the mind-bending logic from the pulpit that your purported preciousness was inherently evil and unclean. Afterall, you're a copy of the one who tempted Adam in the garden and caused the ultimate cataclysm of creation, eliciting God's wrath as he ushered in the birth, suffering, and death of all humanity. I was taught that you are a temptress who leads all to destruction. If "the natural man is an enemy to God" then the natural woman is his nemesis, his arch enemy. Society doesn't trust you. Church leaders don't trust you. God himself doesn't trust you. How could I? I wouldn't. I obeyed the voices of others and I thought I was happy.

As a result, I didn't listen to you.

I didn't want to claim you anyway. The most revered of Mormon scriptures taught me your Brown skin was a curse. Our indigenous ancestors were so wicked God made them "dark and loathsome," marking them as unworthy to mix their blood with his righteous "white and delightsome" true followers. In 1965, our parents somehow defied the church's warning against interracial marriage and we came to be. As a descendant of Mexican immigrant grandparents on our dark-skinned father's side, and of English Mormon handcart pioneers on our fair-skinned mother's side, you embody the blessed and the cursed. Being Brown on the outside but feeling white on the inside, we don't fit anywhere, especially the church. Two decades ago a child in your Provo neighborhood pointed at the skin on your arm. "Dirty," she'd said. She believed it. I believed it. Since I couldn't shed you I tried harder to make up for both of us, being always more obedient, righteous, and fit for God's kingdom. We married a priesthood holder in the temple and created an eternal family. You carried and birthed children with hair, skin, and eyes shades lighter than yours. When we lived in Texas, a stranger asked, "Aren't you glad he's so light?" pointing at our blonde-haired blue-eyed baby son. It turns out Brownness is looked down on beyond the church, out there in the world. As the scriptures prophesied, because of my faithfulness, my children were the promise of the Book of Mormon coming true. They were spared my burden of God's curse and could pass. I was faithful and I thought I was happy.

As a result, I didn't accept you.

For four and a half decades you and I went on this way, intertwined yet apart, as we dutifully filled our roles as daughter, wife, and mother, serving in callings and following directives. And, according to church teachings, we would continue this way until the day I discard you upon death. And, as promised, if I proved myself good enough, we would be reunited on the morning of the First Resurrection, you in your perfected form. I sometimes wondered if you'd still be Brown or if my white God would perfect that in his image, too. Then, I would finally be happy.

But something was happening, had been happening for a long time, something deep below my awareness. Tiny cracks began appearing in the solidness of my beliefs. As massive and slow moving as tectonic plates, my long-held mental frameworks slowly shifted, changing the landscape of my consciousness. It was through these fractures that I began to see you, feel you, marvel at your innate knowing. Creating and birthing children can do that.

But it was in the wake of the death of our third child that I became aware of your intelligence. I tuned into the steadiness of your heartbeat, your will to keep breathing when I didn't think I could go on. You carried us through and continued to patiently hold and support us. You waited so patiently over the years until I was ready to finally be in a place to listen. When enough of the barrier between us had crumbled, you revealed what you'd been holding so deeply in the subterranean layers below my knowing: you're gay. *I'm* gay.

This revelation ripped through me like a betrayal. I had been vulnerable and trusting, starting to believe you to be good—and you show me this? At the same time it felt like another piece of you and me aligned and clicked into place. I wasn't sure I could survive the implosion of the family we created, shattering the worlds of our children and heartbroken husband. But as painful as it was, stronger still was the deep magnetic pull toward this further inner alignment. Full embodiment became my true north. And miraculously, the more vulnerable, honest, and authentic I was, the stronger and more connected I became with others.

It is now my responsibility, my sacred work, to bring us together. I'm learning how to be fully human and inhabit all your bits and parts, listen to your messages, and accept you as you, my feminine, queer, Brown body. To do this I have to continue unlearning what I've been taught, decolonizing my mind, body, and spirit. This process is painful and necessary. Each gain is hard won. I peel back and explore every layer of mental, emotional, and physical pain, sorrow, and anger (the last of which I'm just starting to recognize and allow). My continuing studies on stress and trauma teach me that our health and future depends on us working together to heal these wounds.

I now understand that reclaiming all of ourself is defiance against oppressive institutions and structures. Deepest pleasure and profound joy are acts of resistance.

So, you and I, (us, we) will continue to reflect, create, wonder, meditate, feel, howl, appreciate, weep, discover, revel, stretch, and breathe our way toward each other, toward love, toward home. Wholeness is revolution.

A REVELATION

ERRAN SPEAKER

We looked over at the Federal Reserve building, then back at the app.

"I don't think they're having church meetings here," Janet said, smiling from the driver's seat. The light summer breeze ruffled her hair through the open window. My window was rolled up because I had been rather careful with my hair that morning and didn't want it ruffled at all.

I smiled back, albeit a little weakly. Neither one of us were from the area. We had only just met that weekend, and here I was dragging her around, looking for a church meeting I wasn't entirely sure she wanted to attend. This was our third unsuccessful try. Maybe we had struck out.

We looked back at the phone. 110 South State. We looked again at the blocky, red-brick government building on the corner. Clearly, the app was possessed. Either that or the transphobes were right and Jesus really did *not* want us going to church after all, whatever the new policy said.

"Maybe we should just stop and go do what everyone else is doing?" I asked, trying to leave her a way out.

"Let's try one more!" She did a 4-lane U-Turn. Janet was clearly braver than me.

While she was humming and following directions, I worried again if this was the right thing to do. Was our apparent inability to find an LDS meeting house in Mormonville, Utah, a sign my prompting had been wrong? Should I just accept that I had made a mistake? Or should I endure to the end despite the obstacles? The North Star conference was over. Maybe I'd exhausted my spiritual allowances.

The conference had been amazing. From my first experience at the opening social to the concluding testimony meeting. I had met more Mormon trans women, and more Mormon queer people generally, than I had known existed. Along the way, I started asking God where I should go and who I should sit by. The nudges I received led me to a lunch table where the father of a trans child told me I changed his entire perspective. That was nice, and I felt like I had been the answer to someone's prayer. It also led me to sit next to a trans sister who told me how she had just started traveling from ward to ward, a different one every month, attending for a few weeks and then, on fast Sunday, bearing her witness that she is a beloved daughter of God. As she told me her story of the dozens of wards she had been to, I found myself in tears. The overwhelming witness of the Spirit to me was that sometimes we start down a path without knowing where or how it will end, hoping and trusting in God to prepare the way before us. That conversation had been an answer to one of my prayers.

And all those wonderful experiences had led me to another prayer at the end of the conference, and a desire to seek out and attend a local family ward. Janet had agreed to drive us. There's something in me that apparently doesn't mind attending church as a woman, but recoils from purchasing an Uber on Sunday.

"We're here!" Janet said, turning into the parking lot. I might have been imagining it, but her smile suddenly looked a bit more strained.

"It says they started almost an hour ago," I noted, pointing at the app.

"It hasn't been right yet!" She grinned with a little more humor this time. "Besides, maybe they do second hour first and we can just sneak in for sacrament meeting?"

My heart was pounding a little. This was an actual LDS ward building with all the classic trimmings visible on the outside. Probably on the inside too, but it wasn't really the building I was worried about.

Janet already had her door open, so I squelched the question I had been asking and followed her. As we walked through the two sets of glass doors and into the foyer, the sound of someone talking over the pulpit reached us from the open chapel doors and the foyer speakers at the same time, blending oddly and making it difficult to hear what was being said.

"Are we going to Relief Society?!?" I finally managed to ask as Janet paused.

"It's still sacrament meeting," she replied.

That *hadn't* been what I asked. In fact, it was *why* I asked. Clearly, they weren't doing second hour first.

"Just be polite and don't acknowledge anyone being rude." Janet sounded like she was telling herself more than me as she moved to the open chapel door. And then, to my horror, inside. In the middle of the concluding speaker's testimony, and straight to the long middle row of pews. I was shocked to find myself, lemming-like, about two steps behind her. I wasn't sure if I was more scared of what we were doing or more worried about being left alone. The concluding speaker stopped just as I was taking my seat, sweeping my dress beneath my crossed legs, and clutching for a hymnal. Maybe no one had noticed. I kept my eyes down to preserve that frail belief and vaguely hoped that if everyone just focused on the hair and the dress I might pass for a moment.

After what seemed a dreadfully long time, a member of the bishopric took over the microphone at the pulpit, thanked all the speakers, and introduced the final hymn and benediction. I started to breathe again as the opening strains of "I Stand All Amazed" filled the space. Looking up, finally, I was able to take in the chapel more fully. The slightly off-white paint, green upholstery on pews and chairs, and stained wood accents overhead, on the walls and across the front of the stand. The stained-glass windows flanking the pulpit were a nice touch, I thought absently as my fingers fumbled for the right page and my voice lifted in the familiar words of the opening lines:

I stand all amazed at the love Jesus offers me,
Confused at the grace that so fully he proffers me.

I turned to Janet, sharing the hymnbook, and automatically moving to trace the words across the page with a long fingernail lacquered in light pink lilac.

Oh, it is wonderful that he should care for me
Enough to die for me!
Oh, it is wonderful, wonderful to me!

I felt the easing of my heart as we sang, felt the warm glow of

being here and singing with the congregation in this familiar setting. There are those who don't want us here, and there are many
who just want us to go away. Most of us do eventually. I had been
going to queer-affirming churches for years, looking for, and finding,
fellowship and the spirit. This was different. This was the church I
had grown up in. Not this specific ward, of course, but definitely a
cookie-cutter impression.

> *I marvel that he would descend from his throne divine*
> *To rescue a soul so rebellious and proud as mine,*
> *That he should extend his great love unto such as I,*
> *Sufficient to own, to redeem, and to justify.*
> *Oh, it is wonderful that he should care for me*
> *Enough to die for me!*
> *Oh, it is wonderful, wonderful to me!*

Would the people around me be able to see it? I wondered. Would
they know how deeply God had touched my life, unusual though my
path might be to them? Or would they look only at the outside? I'd
felt prompted to seek out the meeting. I hadn't gotten any reassur-
ances it would end well.

> *I think of his hands pierced and bleeding to pay the debt!*
> *Such mercy, such love and devotion can I forget?*
> *No, no, I will praise and adore at the mercy seat,*
> *Until at the glorified throne I kneel at his feet.*

As the hymn concluded and I gently closed and put away the
hymnal in its little rack on the back of the pew, the individual offering the closing prayer stepped forward. Somehow, I still had enough
peace to focus on the prayer, particularly the words "please help us
to feel thy spirit in the classes being taught today." That peace lasted
right up until everyone said "Amen" and started standing up.

"Do you still want to try for Relief Society?" Janet asked, looking
at me over the top of her glasses.

"Do you think we should ask someone if it's ok?"

"No," she said firmly. "If we go, we just walk in. If they don't want
us here, they'll have to ask us to leave. Visitors welcome!" She was
definitely a bit more on edge than she had been previously. Would
the sisters be all right with us staying? More to the point, would the
priesthood leadership? We both knew stories that didn't end well.

I became aware of someone stopping by the end of the pew where I was sitting and looked up to see a woman smiling down at me. She had short, graying hair and a warm, inviting smile. Her taste in clothing and accessories was flawless.

When I'm sitting down and no one has heard me speak yet, I can occasionally pass enough to leave room for doubt. Once I start talking, there's no question anymore. I gave her my very best "just-us-girls" smile. Janet leaned forward to do me the favor of speaking first. She wasn't fast enough.

"Welcome to our ward! I'm Sister Kay, the Relief Society President. It's so nice to have you visiting us today!"

I sat there, stunned. This was not what I was expecting. Could we possibly be passing? Janet, maybe, but …

Next to me, Janet spoke up: "Thank you, it's wonderful to be here."

"Will you be joining us for Relief Society?" she asked expectantly, still looking at me as I tried to do my best impression of not looking like a deer caught in the headlights.

"We were just talking about whether we might do that or go catch up with some friends," I said, looking to Janet. I was still stuck in the mindset of wanting to give Janet a way out, and at the moment I wasn't entirely certain I didn't want her to take me up on it.

Sister Kay actually seemed a bit sad at the hesitation. "I hope you will come, we would love to have you," she said earnestly, laying her hand on my shoulder in a kindly gesture of affection. Most people won't touch a trans woman. Certainly not with warmth and friendship. I yielded.

"We'd be happy to," I said.

"Good! We meet at the back of the building. Just out the doors and to your right." You could hear the genuine gladness in her voice. "This is Sister Johnson; she can help show you the way. I'll be along in just a few moments." She smiled again with real pleasure as she waved a cheerful mom with long curly hair into place.

I stood up and began exchanging pleasantries as we walked toward the door. It wasn't until I was actually in the foyer that I realized Janet wasn't with me. I almost panicked.

"I'm sorry, I seem to have lost my friend," I said, pausing to look around, my concern spiking sharply.

"I think she went the other way around," said a short blonde sister who suddenly appeared at my side. Her grin was contagious. "Are you coming to Relief Society with us? It's right this way down the hall."

And suddenly it seemed like the hall was filled with sisters, chatting and catching up, stopping to say hi and introduce themselves or be introduced by one of the two sisters with me, asking my name and welcoming me. I did my best to smile and greet each one, trying to remember their names and knowing they were fading away without a trace. At some point I was handed off to an absolutely charming sister who introduced herself as Sister Reynolds. Her white hair was perfectly coiffed and she gave off the most wonderful vibe, full of humor and intelligence.

We had rounded the corner in back where my internal map of a standard LDS meeting house told me the Relief Society room must be. This particular building had eschewed the classic carpeted wall for concrete blocks painted a not-terribly inviting blank white, but at last I could see the door coming up on the right.

The door to the left opened and a man stepped through. The little vestibule behind him had doors opening on to other offices, but I couldn't immediately tell if they were bishop and clerk offices or stake offices. Everyone had halted and I suddenly realized it was because I wasn't moving. He looked up at me. I'm 5'12" when I'm not wearing heels and I had worn heels today.

"This is Sister Speaker," said Sister Reynolds. "She's joining us for Relief Society today."

The man hesitated, then put out his hand. "Welcome," he said. I held my hand out for him to take, murmured something, and then was swept into the Relief Society room.

The room had two doors, one to either side in back. At the front was the classic chalkboard, four-legged table, small podium, and a vase of flowers on a lace doily. There was a piano to one side and the upholstered and padded folding chairs were arranged in a fan shape of three distinct sections, with a small aisle running between them from the door down to a clear space marking the front. The room was already crowded with sisters finding seats and catching up with each other. A giggle from the other side of the room drew my attention just in time to see Janet entering through the other doorway, with her arm wrapped around that of a sister in a blue dress.

"Is this ok?" asked Sister Reynolds, gesturing to a seat in the front row and preparing to sit down. I absolutely would have taken the farthest back corner if I had thought about it before right then, but here we suddenly were and I really didn't want to make waves, so I just sort of went with it. Janet sat down on Sister Reynolds's other side and they immediately struck up a conversation, occasionally including me though I was mostly content to just follow along.

"May I sit here?" I looked up to see Sister Kay beaming down at me again.

I smiled back. "Of course!"

As she settled into her chair the teacher at the front of the class picked up a microphone. "Welcome everyone, it's so lovely to have you all here today."

I sat there, at the front of the room, listening as the announcements were made and a little flyer was passed out. It was incredible just to be present. To hear the soothing voices of the women sparkling around me, the little witticisms exchanged as they discussed past and upcoming events. I'm not sure what it was, maybe just the room full of higher-pitched voices, but I began to relax. I felt embraced. I felt welcomed. The tension just flowed right out of me and was replaced with peace.

"Our lesson today is from Jeffrey R. Holland's talk 'Fear Not—Only Believe.' And I just want to begin by saying something I feel is so important. Every one of us is a needed part of the Kingdom of God. Every single one of us. No matter who we are or what we have been through, we are all needed, individually." The opening caught me off guard, and for a moment I wondered if our teacher was trying to use inclusive language deliberately because we were there. But no, she was speaking to everyone present. And the sisters responded from the depths of their hearts. The lesson unfolded as they poured out their experiences dealing with grief, shame, depression and even feelings about suicide. It was a tender environment. The spirit was very much present, and I had tears in my eyes as they shared their stories and their feelings. But when the teacher asked us "What does it mean to be committed to life?" I cracked.

As a very young child, I lacked the vocabulary to describe what was happening to me. I was physically, emotionally, and verbally discouraged from expressing myself. I learned to bury my thoughts and feelings. I learned shame. I believed the world would be better off without me because I was a poison and a blight. I was caught trying to take my own life when I was ten years old. My parents sent me to a therapist, and when the therapist asked me what was wrong, I lied—because I knew no one could ever know who I really was. Sometime after that, I became committed to enduring, to going back home on the Lord's timetable and not my own, but that isn't the same as being committed to life.

I was sobbing, as silently as I could. Sister Kay put her hand on my shoulder, comforting me.

Sitting in that Relief Society class on that beautiful summer Sunday, those sisters ministered to me whether they knew it or not, with their welcoming smiles and kind words, with their openness and acceptance, and with their stories and honesty. They spoke to me with love, compassion, and acceptance, and I received a glimpse of joy reflected in their love.

TO EVA

EMMETT PRECIADO

I look at old pictures of me now, and I can see how much I was overcompensating just to fit in. It's like I was pretending to be a character, playing "dress-up" every day. It was so exhausting.

I don't talk about it as much as I used to, but I think I need to start again. I grew up in the Mormon Church, I did my best to be as "righteous" as I possibly could. I served a mission because I wanted to help people but also prove my faith and maybe even have my attraction to women taken away. I also thought I wouldn't feel like a boy trapped in a woman's body anymore.

Those two things did not happen.

I did, however, gain an incredibly strong relationship with God, and I know that He loves me. He or She created me. And for anyone who is figuring out how to be true to themselves while also navigating religion or spirituality, I will say this. It is 100 percent okay for you to be *you*. Religion tried to put me in a box and made me believe I wasn't good enough. In fact, I was told I shouldn't exist. But I know this is not true. We are beautiful. Do not let anyone dim your light.

I don't hate "her." I don't hate my past. She is the reason I'm alive and happy today. She fought for my existence, even when she wanted to give up.

Do I ever want to go back to living my life before my transition? Hell no. But if I could go back, I would be kinder to her and give her the warmest embrace. Because she didn't do anything wrong. There was never anything wrong with her.

She just ... wasn't me.

Thank you, Eva. Thank you for not giving up on me. Thank you for standing up for yourself and for being strong enough to push past the fear and the hate that surrounded you in 2015. I love you so, so much.

BREATHING ROOM

AISLING "ASH" ROWAN

for Cosette West

I used to be small.

Smallness *defined* me.

For a lesson on the word "inversion," my dear third-grade teacher, Mrs. West, received my permission to hold me up by my ankles in front of the class (thus inverting me). We all erupted in gleeful delight as I dangled. Another day, a bottle of lotion had lodged itself upright inside Mrs. West's desk drawer and jammed it mostly shut, so she asked me to reach in and remove the wedge.

Both times: *since you're small.*

Small is no bad way to be. When I think about smallness, I envision tiny creatures in a fantasy illustration—mice in knitted jumpers, taking cover beneath mushrooms or inside their tree-root dens, cooking stew and tea. Small is cozy. It's safe. For a while, I found it comfortable to be thin and little.

But somehow, gradually, I felt the need to stay small. To shrink down and stay crunched into a container that constricted my limbs into my ribcage.

There's a running in-joke within the trans community about the "dysphoria hoodie." It's a staple in many of our outfits, regardless of season, serving as shroud for these bodies that we uneasily inhabit. Sure enough, my ninth-grade signature look included hunching into a National Junior Honor Society zip-up jacket, with mousy hair pulled taut into a ponytail. Color had seeped away from the rest of my wardrobe, leaving behind only a muted spectrum of mostly grays, blacks, or the darkest blues. *Please don't perceive me,* I incanted subconsciously every time I got dressed. *Let me hide and fade away. May these clothes completely engulf me and make me vanish.*

As it turns out ... leaving the closet also made more room to breathe.

Exhale. An explanation about my new name and pronouns has been shared on Facebook. My brother reacts with a heart. He'll ask me about it again later during a family temple visit, casually wondering what it must be like to feel othered in these starkly gendered spaces. I'm taken aback; how had he even thought to ask that? The words gather me in and move me, from blending in invisibly to the warm spotlight of being seen.

Exhale. On my TV screen, a montage sequence plays: the angel Aziraphale and the demon Crowley play out their entangled lives, as endearment grows into admiration across centuries. I'm filled with Achillean longing. A few hours later, I drive to my first Pride festival. The city library is decked out in huge vibrant banners. Bright rainbowy booths line the trail through the park, where I meander in a summer swelter. I meet my gender-mentor and friend Kris for the first time in person. I pick out a crystalline pendant to bring home, a pale green. Someone on stage cries out about liberation, and this, too, is breathing room.

Exhale. In my hometown, in a small shop, we approach the checkout counter. "I like your pins!" I gasp, when I notice the cashier is wearing a nonbinary-colored heart.

"Cool shirt," they smile back, and I remember it's printed with "Relient K" repeated in layers, the colors of a rainbow.

In the car, I remark to my kid, "They were a person, like me!" (That's the terminology we use—there's girls and boys and persons.) Then I realize: I'm also speaking with bewilderment to child-me, who lived here nearly two decades ago. *I'm not the only one.*

I'd never realized how often the air had caught in my chest, until moments like these melted away the tension. This is the embodiment of my queer joy—*expansiveness*. It's the sensation of puffing up and out instead of curling in. It's the freedom to move with ease, from finding pronouns in an email signature all the way into the campy flamboyance of a drag show. Joy is an entire spectrum to experience, to feel in my whole body. And there are so many instances when I feel the same as I did in that elementary school classroom, swaying upside-down, overjoyed to see the world from a new vantage point while defying the very forces of nature—and celebrated for it.

Back then, I used to be small. There's nothing wrong with being small, and sometimes, in some ways, I still am. But now, I don't always *have* to be. I can just breathe it all in, living into being the most *me* I can possibly be—and wearing brightly-colored button-ups while I do.

DANCING ON RED-HOT FURNACES

J. ROBYN BYERS

There is a man in aristocratic finery with fire at his fingertips following me.

I shouldn't be surprised, though, considering I created him. What started as a tabletop RPG character evolved into a persona that every day I vividly imagine myself becoming, throwing fireballs, charming unwitting strangers with overwhelming charisma and the sheer weight of self-empowerment. I'm sure I can't be the only autist who dreams of a world where magic is real in a way that makes sense, instead of the confounding sorcery of the average person's sense of social decorum. But when the imaginary friend named Jarin Niranai started talking back, I began to question. Is he me? Is he someone I want to become? Characters and voices whirl through my brain like leaves on the wind, and I can never quite predict when one will reveal itself to be not a leaf, but a seed, touching down just long enough to take root and grow into more than I imagined it could.

But why this one? Of all the people I've made, the voices I've heard and minds I've inhabited, why has he gained almost a mind of his own? Why has he wormed his way out of my brain and into my eyes like a bloody poniard to a Scottish thane-who-would-be-king? Certainly it's the charisma and the confidence. Maybe not the demonic consortium and pledge of allegiance to the Lord of the Eighth Ring. And it can't possibly be the fire that flows from his hands as naturally as breathing.

I hate fire. It's scalding, it's bright, it eats everything in its path with no consideration for the lives it consumes. I grew up in California, where we for several summers saw wildfires so close and so choking that my elementary school turned into Brandon Sanderson's

Final Empire: red sun, toxic air, teachers and students staying inside as much as they could out of fear of something too powerful to keep in check. In my teenage years I attended that horrid domain of pyromaniacs called Boy Scout camping trips, where more masculine young men than me made games of seeing how close they could stand to the blaze, and laughing at me for panicking when, even in the midst of a considerable downpour, I panicked when the bonfire managed to momentarily escape its rocky confines.

Yet this man born of flame and understanding speaks to me, becomes me in my most dire moments. He takes control when I am threatened, fighting back with fire thankfully only metaphorical, defending and protecting me while I shake in the back of my own mind, unable to handle the crisis taking place outside. Slowly I began to understand him and his fire, if not embrace it. It burned down the closet door when I could no longer keep it shut, kept me warm through years of attending a school that hated me and my kind, and it changed to all the colors of the rainbow in the moments when I, finally, embraced fully who I am. When I had my first kiss, a wonderful, indescribably gay kiss, it flared so bright I thought I'd go blind. When another boy told me he wanted nothing more than to have me in his life forever, it flared brighter still. Moment after moment of beautiful fiery light paired with similarly bright flashes of understanding.

Even then, I feared it. Fire is a useful tool, but it is still dangerous. Don't go too far too fast, they all warn, lest it escape your control and begin a catastrophe. I keep the fire close to my heart, but it bucks against the confinement. No, I tell it. Not now. There are times when you're useful, times when I have to fight, but not always. You have to stay down until another one comes.

Jarin was with me one day in the autumn when I walked home from work and felt a tap on the tip of my nose. Another on my shoulder, and a third on the back of my hand. I do love to walk to work in the rain, but this one changed from a pleasant shower to a downpour that threatened the integrity of the grocery bags I carried in my hand. I huddled in an underbridge tunnel and debated with my pyromantic companion whether it was better to wait for the rain to ebb, or risk rushing home through the wet. He held flickering flames in both his hands and said nothing.

And suddenly I wasn't in that tunnel anymore. I was standing in a wide-open field, ten years younger and what felt like a world away, staring up at a dark sky staring at even darker clouds with their deluge of a cargo. At fourteen, I and everyone else in the Meadowview Second Ward got to participate in the cultural celebration to commemorate the dedication of the Gilbert Arizona Temple. The president of the LDS Church himself was going to show up, and our ward had been assigned the Fire Dance.

We weren't the ones with actual fire, obviously; that was left to trained professionals brought in for the occasion. Instead, we had two red-painted sticks. But as the celebration—and Noah's flood with it—began, those sticks became warm lifelines against the cold and rain. When we ran out onto that field as the music began we screamed, and in that moment it had been a scream of defiance against the weather, the world, everything keeping us from dancing peacefully for our prophet. The Fire Dance was supposed to represent Nebuchadnezzar's fiery furnace, and performers were on stage to declare that they did not fear it, for it would never take them. They would never bow to Babylon.

In that tunnel under the bridge with Jarin's fire flickering in my mind, I was ten years and several worlds away from the good little straight Mormon teen boy who danced with wooden fire in the rain, but I still remember the chorus to the closing number to the celebration, and its appropriately ambiguous empowering catchphrase of "Live True." Live true to what? To yourself, obviously, if that self was straight and pious and only had sex with a spouse of the opposite sex you'd married after meeting them at a Fast Sunday Munch 'n Mingle three weeks prior (this is not verbatim). Meanwhile, I'd lived true to Babylon, to the fiery furnace, to an idea that flares out of control and eats everything in its path with no consideration for the lives it consumes. You know, the idea that says that people are allowed to love and be who they are and God is okay with that. It's been a useful tool to fight with, when the usefulness trumps the danger of wielding it so openly.

I ended up braving the downpour to get home quicker; I've never been good at waiting. I had a boyfriend coming over that night to help me cook dinner and I needed the time to make myself presentable. That night, with homemade tikka masala bubbling on the pan and his arms around me, I thought about the fire in Jarin's hands, about the rain, about living true to myself even if that self was Babylon. It was only after he'd left for the night that I realized I'd had it wrong all along. Babylon was a force of tyranny, of compelled obedience, of destroying any who would not bow totally to its whims. Was my fire that? Or was Babylon the school that told me to hide all signs of who I was, the religion that told me that love was something I needed to overcome to get put on the shortlist for heaven?

And if that's the case, what is Jarin's fire? It flares to life from my chest in times when it's needed, golden and black together, but what am I doing with it?

I hated fire. It was scalding, it was bright, and I thought it ate everything in its path without consideration for the lives it consumed. I don't think that anymore. Jarin's fire, *my* fire, is certainly a tool, and it certainly is good in a fight, but that's not everything it is. It yearns to be free not because it's dangerous, but because it's beautiful. I am beautiful. My life is beautiful.

Babylon can be a church. Fire can be a wooden stick in your cold, wet, adolescent hand. Your fictional RPG warlock can be the truth in your mind, not needing to speak, only to show. That the purpose of your fire isn't what you thought. That sometimes, the point of fire is not fear.

Sometimes, the point of fire is to dance.

"OTHER. PLEASE EXPLAIN."

A UNIVERSAL FRIEND

My gender is *peculiar*.

My gender is the delicious moment of hesitation before the cashier decides to use "sir" or "ma'am."

My gender is the delightful moment that follows, right before they apologetically switch to the other.

My gender is leaning against a wall, foot propped up behind me, a green g2 dangling between my fingers like a cigarette, wearing a mustard yellow denim jacket, black t-shirt, light-wash skinny jeans, and black leather hi-top chucks.

My gender is weird earring girl.

My gender is almost impossible to misgender.

My gender is a neatly trimmed beard to masc my remarkably weak chin.

My gender is realizing that actually *I* want to wear my wife's striped cardigan with elbow patches that I've been pestering her to wear more for years.

My gender is play.

My gender is Schrödinger's unopened box.

My gender is trouble. Ya know, the Judith Butler variety.

My gender is snuggling up next to my kids on the couch reading as the early dawn light breaks through our front window.

My gender is not a man, but also not, *not* a man.

My gender is finally wearing whatever clothes I want, regardless of where they're shelved in the store.

My gender is found proving contraries.

My gender is a '90s holographic collectible—images layered on top of one another, one haunting the other at all times, seemingly transforming but really both existing simultaneously as some distinct thing. Perception transforming me.

My gender is absolutely, unequivocally, without a shadow of a doubt, *not* "bud," "buddy," or one of the "buddies."

My gender is trans.

My gender is an optical illusion.

My gender is *dude*, in its true, pure, gender neutral, equal opportunity form.

My gender is the thrill of being asked, "In what ways have you really enjoyed your femininity the most? Like what activities or aspects brought that most forward in a joyful way for you?"

My gender is not a woman, but also not, *not* a woman.

My gender is feeling flirty and queer as I catch myself looking at my reflection in the mirror, feeling more fully myself than I have in decades.

My gender is non-compliant.

My gender is tossing my long hair around, dancing, and belting, "I thought that they were angels, but come to my surprise, they climbed aboard their starship and headed for the skiiiiiiieeeeeees" into a wooden spoon, while I cook dinner.

My gender is trouble. Good trouble.

My gender is reading quietly in the corner.

My gender is rolling up the sleeves of my white-collared shirt after church, unbuttoning it a couple extra buttons, with my cross and Lithuanian amber necklaces swinging out as I lean over.

My gender is me.

My gender is a velvet teal blazer worn over a white v-neck tee paired with berry corduroy pants.

My gender is playful, loving provocation for adherents to the gender binary.

My gender is luxuriating in the jewel-toned polish gracing my nails, stealing awestruck and admiring glances at it throughout the day.

My gender is any and all pronouns, in a chill way.

My gender is rebel. Rebel scum.

My gender is transformative.

My gender is trouble, said endearingly, with a glint in your eye like the small-town girl to the new kid in town.

My gender is delighting in feeling my wife's eyes on me, her girl-friend who looks like her boyfriend from February last year.

My gender is radical, but with a moderate disposition.

My gender is desperately hoping you don't make a Big Deal™ out of it, but also silently begging you to perceive me queerly.

My gender is a '70s space-pirate lesbian.

My gender is queer.

My gender is joy.

THE PLACE IS TOO COOL FOR ME

JOSH HUNTSMAN

This place was too cool for me. I know. There was a sign. Outside the building. It said Josh Huntsman is not cool enough to enter.

Many places have signs like this. Who would manufacture them? Some unethical sign shop making a killing off how uncool I am? How was it that every cool place I wanted to visit, all across the country, had them displayed between rainbow flags and posters for community events? Was it because I was the type of person they were trying to get away from? People like me. The standard-issue, white, cis, balding, clothes-by-Disneyland-and-Hot-Topic (but not the dark and cool Hot Topic, more like the ironic t-shirts for Gen-X dudes who never learned to express themselves Hot Topic), home-decor-by-Walmart kind of guy?

I recognized the physical manifestations inside my body of panic and started with the learned coping skills. Deep breaths. Positive self-talk. Making all my therapists proud.

There is no sign, I say to myself. *They aren't judging you. You belong here as much as anyone.*

What about the fact that you drove more than an hour to come here? They'll think you're desperate, I say.

I don't reply. The thing about me is that I am a real asshole. When I argue, I tend to get really judgy and *italicky*. I turn all Fox News and just try to bury the truth with every hot-button issue I can think of. Something usually sticks.

Hey, remember how people always seem to make fun of bald men? That's funny, right? Hey, you're bald too, right?

I don't reply.

Also, you are never, in a million years, going to get their pronouns right. I'll be surprised if you remember their name at the end.

I always eventually hit where it hurts. I was genuinely scared of this.

I park the car—the huge, friendly-looking SUV my kids named Booster—on the side of the road behind where all the bicycles and electric vehicles are parked. I am sweating. I have pit stains.

I text my wife: I'm scared as hell. I don't know if I can do this.

She texts back: You'll be great. Breathe. Have fun!

I breathe.

She is going to leave you and you will deserve it, I say.

I don't respond. I walk into the tea shop. I have never been to a tea shop before. It was comfortable and neighborhoody. It smelled amazing. Amazing. It was exactly the kind of place I always imagined—a comfortable place to hang out with an assortment of interesting friends.

It's so sad you never, ever, had a place like this, I say.

I don't reply.

Wow. You are by far the oldest person here, I say. *It's not even close.*

I am right. I am also the only one who wore a giant neon sign that says "Imposter" on it. That is bound to attract the eye. Why do I carry it, you ask? I can't help it. It's connected to my shirt and skin and mind. There is a whole industry of demotivational signage dedicated to me not being cool.

I breathe.

The man arrives at the counter and asks what I would like. My brain does the thing it did the first time my post-Mormon ass went into a coffee shop. It freezes in a moment of infinite possibilities but without the slightest clue as to how to proceed. I should have done some research, but I thought I could maybe just say "one tea please" and that would work.

I don't say anything for too long.

"I'm waiting for someone," I say. I am handed a menu. It is of no help to me. I don't even recognize most of the words.

Suddenly a heavenly chord played on an out-of-tune church piano heralding the return of the Still Small Voice.

"You can walk away right now," the Still Small Voice whispered while a way-too-slow version of the most racist part of "Follow the

Prophet" played in the background. "It's not too late. Go back to Booster and drive home to your wife and kids. You don't belong here. Go back to Booster."

I don't reply.

Everyone in the place has visible tattoos except me. I pull out my phone and look at their photo from their dating profile. They look like what you would find under the definition of the word "cool" in a hypothetical dictionary written by myself at age sixteen. Short punky purple hair. All piercings and tattoos and defiance and authenticity. We chatted online for weeks. They smelted. They knew all about edible plants. They wrote self-affirming sex-positive narratives about themselves. They loved Terry Pratchett. They were a veteran. They were very proud of their Native heritage.

It doesn't matter how many times you call them "they" in your mind, you are going to get their pronouns wrong, I say.

I don't reply.

I see them walking up the road in the hot sun. They look less polished than their profile pictures. They did not dress to impress. They wore what they had on.

I'm judging, I say. I imagine my therapists politely clapping for me.

You are not judging. You are right. Look at them.

No. I'm judging, but I'm stopping now.

You're a phony, I say. *This isn't you. You aren't fooling anyone.*

They look frazzled. Eyes stormy. Walk brisk.

The church piano pounds louder in my head. "You need to get in Booster and go home to your wife and kids," the Still Small Voice repeats. "Nothing that happens after this will be good."

Yeah, I say. *I might drink tea.*

That shuts up the Still Small Voice, and, mercifully, the piano, for the rest of the day. For a moment, my blood stops pumping as I realize I really did forget their name. I frantically look down at my phone again to try and remember. It's J.

J and They. J and They. Don't forget. Please don't forget. Worst case scenario? Avoid all pronouns.

We make eye contact before they walk into the place. I smile. They grimace.

Oh god, they're disappointed, I say, triumph in my voice. *Of course they are. Look at you, you old, bald, fat, loser. You thought you could fool them?*

I need to assume the best, I say, but I don't really mean it. I'm sunk. My heart is wood. Maybe I will randomly pass out and then they (rhymes with J) can take the opportunity in the chaos of the aftermath to walk away and I only suffer minor embarrassment. Maybe the ground will open and swallow me up so I won't have to deal with anything ever again.

I *could* fake passing out. I did it once in elementary school and I could do it again. It's 90 percent mental. I prepare.

J is in front of me now. I see their face switch gears and a smile comes up that effectively puts a stop to my plan of fake passing out.

"Hi," they say. "It's so good to finally see you after messaging for so long."

You know, the last time you dated, I said (To myself. Let's not get confused in the midst of my narrative concessions here.). *Most people didn't have phones that let them text. You are so old. Way too old for this. This is a standard midlife crisis but you're escalating it to lunatic heights because you are fooling yourself that your wife is going to remain supportive of all this.*

Then I was hit with the online storm. This happens sometimes.

From behind J, I see the waves crashing through the streets, destroying cars, breaking through the turmeric-colored walls of the tea shop, and hitting me full force in the face with the hundreds of posts and comments from Reddit and Facebook. Post after post about couples who tried polyamory and it was almost always the man convincing his wife that she is really bi and let's find a third, but then getting angry when the wife found love elsewhere. Just more stories of men mistreating women. This storm pounded my face, my ears, bloodied my lip, blackened my eyes.

J starts talking. They were just home with an ex-husband who needed some things back from J's place. There was an argument. J was slighted because their ex-husband was minimizing their anger. Soon we move past that, but I'm still fighting with the motherfucking online storm. I'm talking through broken teeth. I'm listening through cauliflower ears.

I point to a random menu item and pay for it. J orders and we sit and talk. My wife has already divorced me, and I cheated on her so she gets the kids. I maybe get to see them on weekends. My son grows up sad and sullen. My daughter rightly realizes—maybe as early as ten, she's bright—that her dad is a loser and stops trying to communicate with me. Maybe I accidentally slip down the white-guy pipeline and became an incel. Maybe I turn into a joke, an old man who—

"Are you alright?" J asks.

"Yeah," I lie.

"Because you keep apologizing and I'm not sure why."

I didn't realize I had been apologizing.

"I'm sorry," I say. J laughs.

I tell J that, although my wife and I had decided to pursue poly-amory a while ago, this was my first real date with someone I was interested in. That this was my first "first" date in more than twenty years and I wasn't sure what to do. That I was sure I was making tons of mistakes.

J touches my arm and smiles. "You can relax," they say. "You are cool."

Everyone tells you to relax, but that's because they think they know you but they don't. Sure, they like the idea of you. The person you show them, but you know that as soon as people learn about you, about the pansexual-ity, if that's even what you are you phony, about the hypersexuality, about who you really are, who would love you?

Sometimes, in high school debate, my opponent would make a statement that let me know I would win. Some factual error or logi-cal misstep. This happened now because I actually have an answer for the question of who would love me. Because of what happened that first time. The first time I ever hinted towards me not being com-pletely straight to my wife, I was met with a solid wall of support and love. Every twist and turn I took to get to this point was met with support and love. Every lie revealed, every misstep, every secret out, it didn't matter.

I finally had an answer to myself. "I trust my wife," I said.

I realize that this may be the first time I've ever really understood the concept of trust.

That shut me up for the rest of the night.

I leave the pocket dimension I keep in my head for just such conversations and fully join J in the real world for the first time that day.

I breathe. I breathe. I smile.

The tea is amazing. I only wish I remembered what kind it was.

We talk, we drink tea, and eventually, we leave the shop. We walk. It is going amazing. Amazing. I feel young, but not really. I feel like how I imagined I should have felt when I was young.

Me. I feel like me. Like myself. This hasn't happened often. I feel as good as I have ever felt.

I make J laugh so much they say their "smile is hurting." They talk about so many interesting things. I silently say a prayer of gratitude to Jad Abumrad, Robert Krulwich, and the rest of the *Radiolab* podcast team for giving me so many interesting stories so I can keep up with J's amazingly broad knowledge of the world.

J stops, picks what seems like a random weed out of a flower bed we pass and pops it in their mouth. They hand me a leaf. It tastes like licorice. We get snow cones. We drink from a municipal artesian well.

We go to a park full of weird Mormony statues. Joseph Smith as a sphinx is one of them. J says that old white men living in Utah get weird when they want to create art. This garden was Exhibit A. I know more about Mormon theology and teachings than J does so I am able to solve some mysteries of the garden they had. This is supposed to be the stone cut from the mountain that broke apart the statue from the book of Daniel. Mormons say it represents the nations of the earth being consumed by the gospel. The words on these other rocks are from old hymns the church retired long ago because they were too interesting and out there.

We bond over religious trauma. We bond over political trauma. We bond over COVID-related trauma. I talk about my kids. My wife. J listens and celebrates and commiserates with me. They talk about their mom, the military. How they didn't want to live with cognitive dissonance.

It gets dark and we still walk. Every time we pass one of those app scooters that litter the sidewalks of most major cities, J takes the time to set it upright and place it properly. J stops and checks every pocket they have before finding a few errant quarters to give to a man who asked us for change.

"It's all I have on me," they say.

We talk and laugh and even cry, and then I use the wrong pronoun.

I see their eyebrows clench like a long-forgotten toothache flared up again. I apologize sincerely. They say it's not a big deal. I feel bad for a moment then let it go.

We eventually, after a few hours, get back to where Booster is parked. We do that thing where we stand in front of my car for a good half hour because neither one of us wants the conversation to end. Then we sit on an outside bench and talk for another hour or so because we are adults and get to decide how long we talk for.

I talk about how I'm very painfully new to acting on polyamorous and pansexual feelings and that I kinda feel like an imposter. J tells me that I've always been a part of the LGBTQ community because I've always been pansexual. I don't believe them quite yet, but later I will.

We hug goodbye and promise to see each other again soon. I realize as I feel their body against mine that I have a huge crush that makes me feel silly and young and I don't dare try anything more physical.

I get in Booster and sit and I watch J walk away.

I call my wife.

"How did it go?" She sounds excited like she sounds when she talks to her friends about their dates and lives. It's new, tonight, for her to talk this way to me. After twenty years it's something new. It feels comfortable and exciting at the same time. I gush about my crush and I'm more sincere than I've been in a long time. I don't hold anything back. When I am finally done, my wife giggles.

"Are you sure you are fine," I say. "I trust you but—"

"But you need reassurance. I understand," my wife says. "I love you and everything is great."

And I believe her. And everything is great.

OUR LITTLE ZION

SKYLER

The baby wakes up crying. I end the sleep timer on my phone and check when she last ate. Four hours. She's hungry.

Clocking out of work, I set my laptop aside and head up to the nursery. A detour to turn on the light and to assure her that I will be back with food. She wriggles in happiness in seeing me, her dad, after waking up alone after a long nap. A joy I never believed possible for me warms my heart.

But I must leave her for a moment as her food is in the kitchen. Her cries continue as soon as I leave the room because she is too young to understand my assuring words that I will be back with food. I warm up a bottle, making sure that it is warm enough to her liking but not hot enough to hurt her. Eager to bring what my daughter both needs and wants, I rush to the nursery as soon as that sweet spot is reached.

She's old enough now that seeing the bottle causes her to stop crying and give another happy wiggle. I grab a bib and a burp cloth before lifting her from her crib and settling down with her in the rocking chair. Taking too long to settle in will earn another cry, but it is quickly quieted by putting the bottle in her mouth.

She loudly gulps down her first mouthful and it somehow sounds like a sigh of relief. The tension in my body caused by her earlier cries melts away and we enjoy the moment as we stare into each other's eyes.

As her happy gulping noises continue and she begins staring around at the things in her room, I pull out my e-reader. Reading is a lot more enjoyable now that there are so many books with queer protagonists. It is surprising how much representation has improved my joy in reading.

151

When she is done ogling the star light fixture and lamp, she reaches for my face. I let her explore my chin and jaw, hoping to never be the one to squash her curiosity or confidence. There is no harm or danger in letting her learn the connection of what she sees and what she feels, even if it means I get a few more pimples from second puberty.

The nursery rumbles as the garage door opens underneath us. My smile impulsively grows, knowing that my husband is home and will soon be reuniting our happy family. My daughter notices the change on my face, but I don't see my joy reflected in her face until the nursery door opens and she sees him standing in the doorway.

Our baby stops eating and wiggles because having both dads in the room at the same time is too exciting to continue such a mundane task as eating. Our happy family together for the evening. My husband greets us both with a kiss and we exchange words about dinner. Today our daughter had a good eating day, so he goes to make dinner while I convince her to finish the bottle. But it is comforting to know that he would switch jobs with me if it had been a rough day with our baby.

After dinner, we prepare for an outing. Light fixtures and fireplaces have been fascinating to our daughter, so we think Christmas lights will be even more awe-inducing. We load her into the car and go to our city's drive-through light display.

I'm the one driving as the anxiety about having her out of her car seat would be too much for me to be able to enjoy the experience. Part of being a parent is that you won't always be able to watch the joy you bring your child, but that it is still worth it to know that your child is happy. Luckily, my husband captured a picture of her with her hands supporting her on the window as she looks out to a colorful display, her eyes full of wonder and her mouth open in admiration. Proof that it was just as magical for her as we hoped.

We return home and I am soothed by the homeyness of our house. The light blue or purple paint (depending on the light) where once dark gray paint sat chipped and gloomy. Paintings hung on walls that were bare for several years. The sky blue of the nursery covering the putrid green that plagued the spare room until we turned it into a nursery. A structure that once was merely utilitarian turned into a place of joy.

It's my husband's turn to feed her and I finish cleaning up dinner. A new dishwasher was another addition before the baby came. It has saved many arguments as we can simply place things in instead of fighting over what level of rinsed was required to come out clean once the dishwasher as old as we are was done.

I rejoin them in the nursery with the Book of Mormon. We pray and read a few verses before sending her to bed. A kiss on the forehead from each of her dads before we turn out the lights and leave her to cry for five minutes before she falls asleep after a long day.

My husband and I head downstairs to wind down from our day, putting on the next episode of whatever we've been watching. Some days we play video games together, others we do our own separate unwinding activities, but regardless we are together in the same room and not alone.

As we get ready for bed, I appreciate the hard work we put in to gut and renovate our bathrooms. The master bathroom that once was a barely usable narrow hallway; now it fits a double shower and double vanity, so we no longer have to take turns showering or brushing our teeth. It is a reminder, like the scars on my chest, that my life is my own and I don't have to live with something that isn't working for me.

"Adam fell that men might be and men are that they might have joy" (2 Nephi 2:25) in the here and now as well as in the hereafter because "that same spirit that doth possess your bodies at the time that ye go out of this life, that same spirit will have power to possess your body in that eternal world" (Alma 34:34). If I don't enjoy my life now, it will be even harder to learn to love it as a spirit.

Climbing into bed with my husband, I try to apply the advice of my therapist to reflect on how far I've come instead of obsessing about all the things I still wish to change. As I cuddle close to my husband, I think about the little Zion we've created in this house for our little family. It is happier than any future I ever imagined for myself growing up, and we built it together.

GIDDY HEADY GREEDY HEEDLESS

BECCA APPEL-BARRUS

Love and joy are locked in a death grip in Mormonism. Joy is a fruit of the Spirit, and the right kind of love brings the right kind of joy. Brotherly love, godly love, and even carnal love all have a place in the plan (with the caveat that you have to have them in the right place at the right time).

As a kid with undiagnosed depression, I became obsessed with joy. When I finished rereading the Book of Mormon for the dozenth time and started over again, I circled every single reference to joy or happiness in fine purple pen. Eyes drooping after yet another long, exhausting day of being a teenage human, I hunted for any clue that would tell me how to be in the right place at the right time to be fully immersed in a deluge of True Joy.

If my life could be enjoyed as well as endured, I wanted in on it. I'd been happy, but I wanted the indescribable joy felt by the people eating the fruit of the Tree of Life in Lehi's dream. I wanted the kind of elation that caused Alma to straight up pass out when he met up with his mission buddies. I wanted something to make me excited to be on earth, rather than being one of those Mormons who does all the right things, tapping their foot and looking at their watch until the Lord sees fit to take them home.

I wasn't expecting for the Lord to reward my zealous studying and longing with several well-placed nudges until I ended up in a literal deluge without an umbrella, a girl I'd barely met sticking her pianist's fingers into the cracks of my aloof façade and worrying at them until more and more of me was exposed. As much as I didn't want it to be true, this blind step into letting her see me was what I'd been missing.

Falling in love with this girl made me want to live.

I wasn't actively suicidal when we met. Although I couldn't imagine what my life would look like in ten years, let alone fifty, I was young enough to be curious in a detached way about how things would shake out. Any hope I had about the future being more than just a scrapbook spread of grim, frontier woman-style satisfied smiles was muted, flat. I couldn't want too much.

"What do you want to do when you graduate?" She spoke in a careful, deliberate way that I would later learn is to cover up a slight lisp.

We were with a gaggle of girls ducking from awning to awning through the rain on the nearly deserted street, clumping around the menus posted in café and restaurant windows. One of them heard I took Italian 101 and had convinced me to come along to help figure out if "lasagne con ragu di agnello" was a familiar dish.

"I don't know, I haven't thought that far ahead," I said distractedly, hands shoved into my pockets, trying to decide if I could afford a dinner that cost more than five euros.

"On the bus earlier, you said you wanted to be a writer." Her voice was gentle but firm. Holding me accountable, reminding me that my words have value. That someone was paying attention to the bullshit I spouted. "What do you like to write?"

When I defensively said I felt like I was being grilled, she gave a self-conscious little laugh. "My dad's a lawyer. I didn't mean to pry; I just want to get to know you."

She came into my life, talented and beautiful and kind and dorky and painfully earnest, and I wanted her. I wanted her and all of a sudden my ravenous heart wouldn't shut up when I told it we should calm down and be cool.

I didn't feel cool. I felt my inadequacies keenly. I could see who I could be emotionally, academically, spiritually if I buckled down and worked hard. I felt glowy. I felt kinder. I felt like a better person than I ever thought I could. I felt lovesick. I felt hopeless.

I felt like I would sell my mess of pottage a million times over if I could sit next to her on the bus for just a few more minutes.

Oh, I thought when my infatuation crossed into Something Else. When I finally stopped shushing my heart and started listening to what it was screaming. When she told me in a thousand ways that her heart was screaming the same way. *Oh. This is it.*

Although neither of us (even me with my punk posturing) were rule-breakers by nature, we couldn't stop sneaking off together. We weren't even making out. The presence of the other person underscored the beauty of the paintings we saw, the gardens and ruins we walked through, the wet acrid clouds of cigarette smoke on every street corner. It would have been a waste not to see the sights like this.

We'd slip away so she could play ABBA and Flo Rida mashups on the piano, so I could find gooseberry pie so she could properly celebrate Thanksgiving, so we could link arms and slyly mock all the guys who hit on her.

Giddy. Heady. Greedy. Heedless.

"I'd better get going," I'd say toward eleven o'clock, feet planted by the kitchen counter upon which she was perched, a freshly showered, makeupless, radiant queen to whom I would forever pay court. "I'll miss the bus."

She'd pull caramel digestives and a tin of hot chocolate powder out of the cupboard, drop a kiss on my temple, and ask, "How long do we have before the next one?"

Despite our complete and utter absorption in one another often making us late for events or miss them entirely, she was a big planner. We made formal plans and casual ones—"Let's see *The Mousetrap* next Friday" or "After Christmas break, we have to go to Thai Ruby"—hungrily taking over more and more real estate in the other's life.

With every event slotted into my calendar, my life got a little longer. *I can't go into a coma to avoid finals week. We have a picnic planned and I said I'd make her a macaroni salad.*

I loved her. I wanted to live and I was excited about it, not merely resigned, because I wanted to be there to listen as she outlined her latest project. I wanted to rub her sore legs so she could sleep more peacefully. I wanted to make up silly stories to take her mind off the things that made her cry inconsolably.

As I lived for her, I slowly learned how to live for myself.

There's one particular photo of us where it's so obvious that we're in love, I was surprised the Honor Code Office didn't beat down my door and expel me the second it was posted.

We're surrounded by a throng of revelers, coated, booted, and scarved against the northern cold. Her face is raised to the sky, eyes squinting against the force of a dazzling smile, cheeks and nose pink, hair pulled back, one tiny golden lock gone rogue and curled into a perfect spiral at the base of her neck.

I'm staring right at the photographer. There's a smile on my face as well, only it's different from hers. It's self-satisfied, bordering on smug. Like I got the last dessert at a high-end patisserie after standing in line all day. I didn't think I would make the cut before they ran out, but I did and you didn't and I'm going to savor every single bite and I don't care who watches.

I'll devour this unexpected, unearned pastry and I'll lick every single crumb off my fingers and then I'll lick again to make sure I didn't miss anything.

Our arms are wrapped around each other. Warming. Declarative. Possessive.

Her head on my lap, my shoulder, my chest.

Her fingers on my hair, my waist, my lips.

Nothing could touch us and no one else was able to see to the end of the tunnel that was blasted through our hearts. It just kept going and going and we went hurtling through it as fast as we could, screaming into the darkness, exhilarated and exquisite.

We are here!

SECTION 3

JOY IS GRATITUDE FOR HOME

TO DANCE IN THE DIM LIGHT: MEDITATION ON JOY, PART 3

KERRY SPENCER PRAY

On my first date with my wife, I ordered the world's most terrible drink. The thought of it comes unbidden to my mouth, even now, years later. An entirely wrong balance of sweet and sour and tequila, cut with the wrong sort of mixer, served at the worst temperature.

"That is the most awful drink I have ever seen," she said. "And I was a bartender. I have seen some terrible things."

Her arms were covered in tattoos—a naked woman, standing in a tangle of flowers, an infinity blossom on her wrist. The tattoos seemed exotic to me. So foreign, so different from the strict rules of body and appearance I'd grown up with. I still couldn't uncover my shoulders without feeling their nakedness too acutely, without feeling like I was doing something wrong, by existing in plain sight.

"It is the worst thing I have ever tasted," I said. "I don't know how to drink. I used to be Mormon. I don't know what I'm doing." I laughed, with the uncomfortable sort of laugh that comes out on first dates when no one is entirely sure what to do with themselves and their voices come out at the wrong pitch, the wrong volume and speed.

"Here," she said. "You should try this one." She handed me hers. It was a Blue Moon beer, garnished with an orange. The taste was mild and much less horrible than the drink I'd ordered myself.

"Oh, that is not bad," I said. "You're going to have to order me a drink next time, so this doesn't happen again."

"Clearly," she said, "you clearly need the help."

When I was on my own, I started to dance in my kitchen.

I would make myself something with vodka in it. It was never quite as bad as the drink I had on that first date with my wife, who I married years later, but it was never very good either.

I felt like I was fumbling toward something, and I didn't know how to get there. I only knew that every string I cut, disentangling me from the life I'd had before, I felt freer. More able to move.

As I tried to dance in my kitchen, I wanted to think that I looked wild. That if I leaned into the sense of wild, I would find it—the dancing. That I could take laughter and make it motion, spin circles of meaning, say, out loud, to no one in particular in my kitchen, that I was alive, and I *mattered*.

I doubt it actually looked like this.

My wife and I went to a party dressed in cruise gear once, before she was my wife. It was a themed party, and she bought boat shoes for me, and a captain's hat. I wore shorts that were seersucker, with a woven belt. I danced in the middle of the room, even though no one else was dancing. She laughed and recorded me doing it. I watched the video later, in the car when we drove back to her apartment.

"I look like an adolescent giraffe," I said.

"That is not even a little wrong," she laughed.

She opened the sunroof to her car and the cold night air came inside, whipping against my ears in the starlight.

It didn't really matter to me what I looked like as I danced.

I was alive.

I was wearing boat shoes.

She had told me to dance.

And I had done it.

It was the *point*.

"This essay still feels very heavy," my partner said to me.

I sighed, stood up. "I added the chocolate sauce story!" I said.

"You did!" they said. "And I laughed!"

"But it is still heavy."

"It is still heavy."

I looked over at the barn doors, hanging between my dining room and my living room. They were a dark color, not green and not blue. The living room and dining room used to be a single open space. But when the pandemic hit, there weren't enough rooms for everyone to have a place to work.

Our house was a crowded one. My (now ex) husband lived downstairs in the basement apartment. When the world locked down, he was between boyfriends, but his space was still small. Our children were teenagers. My wife used our bedroom as an office space. The only place left for me was the living room, but the sounds of the kitchen would come through the dining room and interrupt the classes I was trying to teach online.

My husband and my wife decided to conquer the problem together. They bought barn doors, assembled them together, and hung them up to surprise me.

I watched them do it, strategizing and conspiring. They would tilt their head in the same way, would move their hands in the same way. When they asked why I was laughing, I confessed, "I am feeling extremely called out by the fact that, no matter the gender, I clearly have a spouse *type*."

They laughed with me.

Our arrangement may be odd, but it is loving.

At Christmas time, we arrange the presents under the tree for the kids. We drink secret midnight (spiked) eggnog as we work together. We have a tradition of celebrating birthdays by the month in addition to the year—100 months, 200 months, 500 months, as many months as days we want to celebrate. We eat dinner together, telling harrowing stories about the seedy gay bar in DC, laughing about how it adjoins to the brightly lit quiet lesbian bar in such a contrast. Our children don't just have a mother and a father like other children. They have more than that.

I'd been taught the only good family, the only family worth striving for, was a nuclear one. Man, woman, their children. That nothing else was worthy of eternity, that anything else was "counterfeit."

But this was my family and I had built it. It was not even a little nuclear, but it was mine and it was *good*.

The doors my husband and wife built for me were heavy.

Something being heavy didn't make it bad.

Sometimes the weight just made it more good.

"Well," I said to my partner. "Then the essay will be heavy."

I don't pray to Father God anymore.

It's not that I don't pray—I do. But my prayers have lost all the formality of my childhood prayers. There is no structure to them. No rigid patriarchal process that must be adhered to, no matter the aching in my heart.

He still watches me.

I feel him, hovering on the edges of my mind. Or spirit. Is there a difference? I can't tell.

I have told him, on more than one occasion, that I can't pray to him anymore. Not like I used to at least. I can't pick back up the structures that were meant to give shape, but only served to smother and confine.

To his credit, he seems to understand.

He seems to know better than me why I can't and doesn't begrudge me for it.

Every now and then I feel him push me forward, like a parent whose baby no longer needs training wheels. He never quite says that he always wanted this for me—this freedom. This celebration of me, for who I am, and not for all the things I am not.

But she does.

Under the moon sometimes I can almost hear her cackle.

In the darkness of the bedroom, I will kiss my partner. When their hands reach for my face, I will see her sometimes then too.

Sometimes she is still the shadow, behind my right (always my right) eye.

Sometimes she is still veiled.

Sometimes she fills me with a rush of the wild kind of love. The kind that says that yearning should be followed, that structures should be left behind, that life should be a *dance*.

Sometimes I fall asleep, hand heavy against the skin of someone I love so deeply. My mind will be quiet. The aching yearning in my heart, quiet.

This, she says to me, in a voice that is never actually heard, but only ever felt. *This peace?*

It is also dancing.

SUNDAY RELIGION

ELI McCANN

It's Sunday morning and my phone starts buzzing. I roll over in bed and reach for it on the nightstand before realizing it's next to my pillow. My husband, Skylar, and I fell asleep watching TikTok videos again last night. My battery is at 5 percent.

I look at the phone to see who's calling me. It's Skylar. I turn my head to look for him and ask why he's calling me from two feet away but then I discover he's no longer in bed. The dogs are missing, too. This happens sometimes when my snoring prompts a mass family exodus to the couch. I always tell him to just wake me up and ask me to leave the next time I'm being disruptive. *They* shouldn't be the ones displaced. He says he doesn't want to disturb me because he knows I need my sleep.

"Yeah," I groan, answering the phone.

"Oh good! You're up!" he says. I can hear water running on his side of the conversation. He and the dogs are in the backyard giving potted flowers that don't belong in the desert life support.

"We've been waiting *hours* for you to come hang out with us," he continues. "The dogs miss you."

I look at the time.

"Sky," I say. "It's 7:04. How long have you been awake?"

He ignores my question and implores me to come outside and sit with him while he finishes applying another iron treatment to a sick wisteria tree that has been destroying a small brick planter box ever since he brought it home five years ago.

I fall out of bed and drag myself to the backyard. He claps and cheers when he sees me like I'm a talk show guest who just walked out to greet the host. I know the applause is mostly facetious, but it

165

always feels a little flattering and I usually fail to resist a smile that lets him know that.

Eventually we change out of our pajamas and into clothes that are barely distinguishable from our pajamas. We begin our Sunday morning walk, a routine, a ritual—I sometimes say I'm not religious, but maybe this sacred practice of strolling hand-in-hand through my neighborhood I love with the person I most admire is religion.

The warm late summer breeze is gliding down the mountains just to the east of our Salt Lake City street, rolling across the swaying lavender packed along and encroaching on the sidewalks. "I wish everything smelled like lavender," Skylar says. He means it. He has filled mesh baggies of dried lavender, plucked from our own yard, and has stuffed them into every drawer in our house. He says he read this would keep linens smelling fresh, but so far the only difference I've noticed is that loose pieces of dried tiny flowers have covered every surface of our home.

We arrive at our corner store and purchase one copy of our city's newspaper after Skylar inspects it to make sure it has all the sections. He never wants to be burned again after that one time we got all the way to our tea shop to read it and he discovered someone had pulled out the opinion columns.

The tea shop opens at 10:00 a.m., and we arrive just in time to see the owner flip over the open sign on the door and wave to us. Skylar orders two different teas for himself because he can't decide which one he wants—the smallest of indulgences. He tries to take a sip and realizes they are too hot. He lets them cool in thoughtless abandonment until they reach room temperature, just like he always does. He acts surprised when this happens, like it's never happened before.

We trade sections of the newspaper back and forth, giving one another recommendations on articles worth reading. Eventually we get up to leave and walk home. We fold the newspaper back into the tidy pile in which it came and drop it at the counter of the tea shop in case someone later that day wants to give it a read. And then we stroll back to our house, hand-in-hand, gossiping about what we just read and looking for landscaping tips from our neighbors.

We take the dogs to the park. The moment we reach for their leashes they start losing their minds. Our smaller dog wiggles so much from excitement that it literally knocks him off his feet. This never stops being cute.

One of the dogs plays fetch and ignores everyone else while the other dog wanders the park greeting every person and animal like he's a mayoral candidate in the middle of a heated campaign. People tell us our dogs are cute. Skylar and I have completely different ways of responding to this. "I know, right?" I say, with enthusiasm, at the same time Skylar mumbles a humble "thank you."

"People probably think you sound arrogant when you say 'I know' to that compliment," he hisses at me.

I disagree with him. "Well, it doesn't make sense to say 'thank you.' I didn't create these dogs. Why should I assume people are giving *me* credit for their cuteness?"

"Exactly!" he responds, his favorite way of pretending he's just won an argument no matter how good the point was that I just made. I sigh. I hate how this always works on me.

In the afternoon I go for a long run and listen to my favorite podcasts while Skylar goes to the gym, mostly to lie on the floor and scroll through reddit. "I was there for two hours but I think I only exercised for about ten minutes," he says to me when he gets home. He claims it's laziness, but I think it's earned fatigue from working so many hours at the hospital this week. "Nah," he protests again. "Just laziness."

I have a theory that he spends so much energy cheerleading everyone he meets that he doesn't have enough left in the tank to do the same for himself. The cheerleading is a superpower he has. I've seen him make flight attendants misty-eyed after stopping them to compliment something they've done. Recently I heard him make a call to our city's parking enforcement office. "One of your employees was giving a ticket next to the library downtown yesterday afternoon and some mean old man started yelling at her. She got in her car and drove away before I could say anything. Will you please tell her I'm sorry that happened and she didn't deserve it?"

Only he could find a way to humanize and side with a glorified grownup hall monitor wandering the city passing out fines.

By late Sunday afternoon I pour a glass of wine and start making dinner. Skylar is a better cook than me but I'm the only one of the two of us who enjoys doing it so I make nearly all our meals. Tonight

I'm cooking a tofu stir fry. We're going through another one of our phases where we think we're vegans.

"We're actually vegans now," I'll say to friends whenever I've unilaterally recommitted us to this lifestyle. Skylar doesn't know I can usually see him out of the corner of my eye sarcastically nodding, his eyes wide open, no doubt resisting the urge to point out I ate meat just that morning.

After dinner we cuddle up on the couch, our two exhausted dogs who sleep all day and have every need perpetually met, slump on top of us and pass out. We start a movie we'll hardly watch as I knit—I'm making another sweater for Skylar, which I will pressure and manipulate him into wearing as much as possible for as long as possible. He scrolls through his phone studying flashcards related to his dermatology residency. I've asked him why he always seems to be studying even though medical school ended over a year ago. "Because I want to be good at my job," he says in a tone that suggests I asked a stupid question.

Around 9:30 we get ready for bed. 9:30. If my much wilder twenty-something younger self could see this, he'd be concerned.

We lie down, the dogs on each side of us. I start scrolling through TikTok, turning the screen so we can both clearly see it, until we doze off and I drop my phone next to my pillow. The battery will be at 5 percent by morning.

There was a time, for many, many years, where I was closeted, afraid, and so very lonely. I believed loneliness would be the blueprint for the rest of my life, and that scared me.

Somehow, against so many odds, that blueprint changed and gifted me the kind of Sunday some people justifiably might consider to be dull. The kind of Sunday where nothing happens, which somehow manages to make it special. The kind of Sunday no child dreams of having some day because newspaper reads over tea and 9:30 bedtimes are too boring to be the subject of dreams for anyone too young to crave that sort of thing.

Even still, I'll wake up next Sunday to a buzzing phone and an empty bed, I'll see who is calling me, I'll remember what day it is, and I'll smile.

Because for me, this is joy.

WORTHY OF LOVE

BLAIRE OSTLER

It wasn't until my own daughter expressed her desires to marry a girl that I began to internalize my own self-worth as a queer child of God.

I recently watched her play with her dolls while pontificating about her future wedding with a girl, and my heart flooded with love. Her innocence, her goodness, her pureness, her beautiful dreams for a happy future were nothing short of celebratory. She had plans, goals, desires, and reasons to live. I had so much love for her that I thought my heart might explode out of my chest. I felt like I understood the scripture "my cup runneth over."

I whispered to myself, "Oh God, I love her so much."

Then, without warning, a voice came to my mind saying, "That's how much we love you."

My eyes widened and filled with tears. I was taken off guard. I rarely invite my Heavenly Parents to communicate with me. I've been hurt too many times in their name to trust those inner voices. I was told "no" by my community for so long that I couldn't imagine myself as worthy of a sacred "yes." Yet, the voice was clear, "That's how much we love you."

With those words I imagined that I was worthy of love and joy.

THE PROPOSAL

JODIE PALMER

I had a near death experience.
Not the emergency room kind,
but the "I don't know if I can make it to tomorrow" kind.

The kind where each breath
is a selfie posted to the Universes social media
confirming … I'm still here

I have a proposal.

Sweethearts, that suffering was just my own soul
rattling the doors and windows of my heart, saying
"I will NOT let you live someone else's life!"

Sometimes it isn't until the house burns down
that we find our way home.

You and I met at NorthStar.
The irony of that is just too stellar.

First—North / Star should have been flashing in neon over your head.
And second—One often meets their destiny on the road taken to
avoid it.
(credit Master Oogway)

I don't know the physiology,
the theology, or the numerology of destiny.

But I have a proposal.

When we open our hands
Life falls in.
And baby, Life is all the things.
Heartbreak, discovery, wrongs, trembling anticipation, peace, pain,
and bliss.

Like the time I cried myself sick
because I smothered that baby chick my grandpa bought me …
trying to protect it through the night.

Or the time you shattered your parents brand new mirror,
then gathered all your pennies to make it right …
but you got whipped anyway.

All the way …

To the time I ran my hand
up and down your leg on our first date.

Which makes me sound fast,

but my girl,
the hardest thing I've ever done
has been to let go of my grip
on survival and open my hands to life.

They say our same-sex attraction
Is a counterfeit love.

But Lassie, when I take your open palm in mine
it feels like a burning star is born
in the darkness between.

I have a proposal.

That's how it actually is.
This is the Big Bang Theory proven true.
They held hands and said, "Let there be light!"

What is counterfeit
is believing our love is so shallow
it only covers mere attraction.

What is good, beautiful, and true
is that love
is the substance of everything

Which is to say …
Our love is real, my velveteen.

You know, it's hard for me
not to think too big about small things.
But even an atom
is actually a whole universe inside.

If a star can be born
between our palms,
there are no small things, my love.

And the thing I am about to propose next
is the least small thing of them all.

Christy Cook Watkins,
We create something beautiful. Life is for us. All of it.
Marry me
and hold my hand forever.

EASY CONVERSATIONS

JACLYN FOSTER

Utah, 2018

It was one of our last weeks in married housing south of BYU campus before moving to the suburbs of Salt Lake. I had just arrived home from a trip to visit my parents, and I knew it had been lonely for my spouse staying behind to work. We cuddled in bed, when our conversation took an unexpected turn. The crux of it was:

"I—I don't think I'm cis. I don't know what yet."

I tried hard not to pause. "Well, I'm bisexual," I said in what I hoped was a reassuringly casual tone, "I'm sure I'll be okay with whatever you land on."

A few days later, we did our makeup together for the Provo Freedom Festival—Queer Meals had set up a flamboyantly defiant rainbow tent along the parade route, and we turned out to help Make America Gay Again. I had ordered a rainbow dress just for the occasion, my pale shoulders burning in the July heat. We posted smiling pictures to Twitter, and my mom called me, crying.

"Of course I still wear my garments," I reassured, not wanting to have this conversation, "The rainbow dress was for the event. Like a costume."

"I have friends who wear Halloween costumes without garments," my mom responded, "that's a personal choice. But you're not wearing your garments in your haircut selfie from the other day either."

Shit. How had she even noticed that—I'd worn that t-shirt over garments plenty of times before. I had lied, again, to avoid a conversation about the church—and not only had it not gotten me out of discussing it, but now she knew I had lied.

I sent my parents a lengthy and remorseful email a few days later.

In answer to prayer, I explained, I was Marie Kondo-ing my relationship with the church. "All my life, anything that made me feel like I'd made you sad, or angry, or disappointed, has been disproportionately painful to me," I wrote. "Making you feel any of these things is my number one fear and I don't understand why no matter how hard I try to figure it out." I tried to explain, "I don't like lying to you ... but I simply wasn't ready to talk about it yet, and I didn't know how to set that boundary without starting a conversation that would paradoxically cross that boundary."

My dad sent an equally lengthy response on behalf of them both. They weren't particularly surprised, and expressed the difficulty of knowing when to say something and when to stay silent. He could relate to the fear of disappointing parents, and asked me not to equate differences with disappointment. A largely accepting email, it turned frustrating towards the end, closing "don't abandon all things that don't immediately yield you joy." I had a lengthy shower argument in my head about the differences between the Marie Kondo method and instant gratification—but I let the topic drop.

Arizona, 2019

"The church doesn't teach that, though," my aunt protested, seemingly perplexed.

"Well not officially, but a lot of people give that impression," my mom explained. I took some selfies on the couch, trying to mentally check out of the conversation I had accidentally started.

I had called a few weeks before my cousin's wedding, knowing I couldn't just make up a convenient excuse to skip the temple ceremony when there were so many willing younger cousins to watch my toddler for me.

"Do you still believe in a higher power?" was her first question when I said I didn't have a recommend.

"Yeah, I still believe in God and Jesus and all that stuff ... I just can't do church anymore." The conversation had gone well, the first time we'd both been emotional in a conversation without making me panic about our relationship.

"I believe progression between kingdoms is possible," she had cried, and I held myself back from asking if she assumed I'd be starting at a lower one. But now with the extended family I was watching her take my side, even if only she and I knew that's what was happening.

The next evening, I found myself alone with that same aunt during the reception. She asked about my in-laws, and I made a reference to my brother-in-law's boyfriend. "He grew up Jehovah's Witness, so he kind of got how hard it was for Luke to grow up Mormon."

"Wait, why was it hard for him? I thought he was closeted until recently," she asked. I did the internal equivalent of a spit take, remained carefully composed on the outside, and set about explaining internalized homophobia. I must have done it a little too well, because she immediately asked with sincere concern, "So how are you doing?"

The previous evening's conversation flashed through my mind. "Oh, I'm good," I lied. She raised her eyes at the blatant contradiction. "Oh yeah?"

"Yeah." My favorite aunt from childhood, and I couldn't even bring myself to have that conversation.

Canada, 2019

"The premier is supposed to be at the barbecue tomorrow," my mom said. "Oh yeah?" "Yeah, they want all the Relief Society presidents to be in the picture to look like the party and the church have women in leadership, I guess."

I gave a polite chuckle, waiting to see where this went.

"So if they're going to make me be in the picture, I was thinking we could go to the mall and see if they have any pride shirts left I could wear."

"Uh … yeah. Yeah that would be great."

Making it through the mall before it closed would be tight. We power walked through stores where I'd searched for a prom dress with sleeves, stores where we'd bought my new post-mission wardrobe. Now they were stores where I'd bought pride gear with my mom. We picked through the sparse end-of-June selection and settled on a gray tee with a small rainbow stripe across the chest. Subtle enough to have plausibly worn by accident, but those with eyes to see would see.

One of those eyes, as it turned out, was my former babysitter. "She asked if I wore it on purpose," my mom related afterwards as we drove out to Kananaskis, "and I said yes. Then she said, 'you know, your talk in stake conference really changed my mind on some things.'"

I watched my mom later, skipping rocks into the river with my daughter as she'd done so many times with me in the same spot. I snuck a quick photo. My mom in her pride shirt.

Canada, 2020

Two weeks was a long time to quarantine. Kya stayed in the U.S., unable to take that long off work. My mom and sister stayed with my grandma so they could keep working their in-person jobs, and my dad and other sister stayed cooped up in the house with myself and a four-year-old with an insatiable need for entertainment. In a rare quiet moment, my dad and I sat in silence in the front room, reading.

You could just tell him about Kya right now, you know, something inside of me thought. After a moment of surprise, I pushed it aside. Of course I couldn't just out my wife without discussing it first. I sat quietly, exploring this new feeling of wanting to bring up a difficult topic unprompted.

When quarantine ended, I extended the vacation, driving to my grandma's cabin in British Columbia for a family reunion. Nobody had originally thought to invite me—I'd missed so many from living in the U.S., even before the pandemic.

"So how come you moved to Montana?" my aunt asked casually. I froze for a moment.

Oh, you know, whenever my wife comes out as trans we wanted to live somewhere other than Utah, so I cross-referenced the Human Rights Campaign's municipal equality index with the cost of living and found this college town. "Oh it's just um … it's really nice there, not as hot as Utah, great scenery … we just kind of figured, with the remote work now, why not, you know?"

Canada, 2021

The same front room. Another quarantine, this time before my sister's wedding. My mom, instead of my dad, on the leather chair— me, in my usual spot on the couch. I don't even remember what we were talking about, but suddenly my mom was telling me about the "trans girl" who occasionally came up in ward council.

"I said, oh she's just turned eighteen, we should welcome her to Relief Society—we've done that for other less active teens before. And Brother so-and-so said, well I don't think she'd appreciate that, she identifies as a boy. So I said, well then we should be welcoming *him* to *elders quorum*." She laughed almost helplessly, frustrated.

I texted the story to Kya, stuck home working again. "So I think my mom will be okay whenever you come out," I concluded.

"Well that's good, at least," she replied.

A few days later, I stood at the top of the basement stairs, my mom almost to the bottom on her way to the food storage room. I had too many secrets, and one had to burble out. "So I haven't confirmed with the OB yet—" My mom turned around. "But you might want to think about doing Christmas in Montana instead this year." She ran up the stairs without fetching her canned goods and enveloped me in a hug.

Montana, 2021

The agreed-upon weekend finally came. I opened my Gmail app that Friday afternoon, meaning to proofread the draft I'd eagerly written months ago. It was brief and matter-of-fact, two short paragraphs to let them know the good news: I had a wife! I'd intended to send it off the next day, but had my first moment of wanting to procrastinate. Rather than letting the nerves grow, though, I entered each person's email address and pressed send before I could dwell on it. Then I texted my mom:

"Sent you guys an email, not bad news just felt like more of an email thing than a family group text thing. When you get it can you check I got all my siblings emails right?"

Her response was almost immediate. The first word I saw was *congratulations*. "Hey I just read it, congratulations to Kya Mae and your family. Love flows better when we can be our true selves." I had expected acceptance by this point—but I had also expected nervousness, a tense protectiveness against the world that I would have to work to not misinterpret as something else.

Kya came out of her office, misty-eyed. "You can't do that while I'm working," she joked. My mom had immediately texted her as well.

Love flows better when we can be our true selves. As I went about my surprisingly normal weekend, that phrase rang over and over in my head. My mom had been talking about me and Kya, of course—but all I could think about was her and I.

A NEW NAME

ARI AHSOKA

I first met Will in 2017, where we went on our first date to get ice cream.

I first started to think about changing my legal name in 2020, roughly a year after I came out as nonbinary.

This is the story of my new name.

Finding a new name isn't easy. Luckily, I had gone by a gender-neutral nickname since I was about five and that name felt like me. But finding a new middle name took me months. It is even harder when you are engaged so you need a new middle name that works with two separate last names.

10/15/2022

I finally submit my change of name form and get my mum to pay the fee (because I have to change it in the state I was born in, but I currently live in a different state).

10/19/2022

I'm on a Zoom call with my social worker, our final session together, when I get the text message: BDMOffice—2:16 p.m. Your certificate has been generated and will soon be delivered by registered post.

They only sent the text twenty minutes ago but I have already opened the tracking link because I am so excited. I'm so excited that I can't stop saying how excited I am. The certificate doesn't have any tracking information yet, in fact it hasn't left the post office.

I think I am going to have a change of name party. My new name is Ari, which means lion in Hebrew and it means eagle in Icelandic. We could do lion trivia. I don't know what you do at a new name party, but I feel like this needs to be celebrated. I didn't have a graduation party or even go out for dinner because graduating uni came with a sting because my diplomas have my birth name on them and uni won't change them. But now that doesn't feel like it matters because in the mail right now is my change of name certificate, hopefully including a new birth certificate with ducks on it. Ducks are my second favorite animal.

I thought they would take weeks to process my change of name and I was worried that they would reject my application because I had accidentally committed a crime I didn't know about, but it only took them three business days. Normally, I hate surprises or things not going how I planned, even good surprises, but right now I am just so happy that I don't care that this wasn't the plan. I've never felt so seen or so me. It is the complete relief that I no longer have to be associated with my birth name. That the HR system at work that I have to look at whenever I submit a timesheet will no longer have my birth name on it. I finally feel like I get to be me. Today, was just going to be an ordinary day. It is overcast and was supposed to rain, which is why I didn't do my washing. Work this morning was okay, except we had a two-hour meeting. But now today feels like the best day of my life, even though it has been ordinary. I can't explain to you how I feel, the pure euphoria of finally being able to be me. Actually, I can. I feel like my new name Ari Ahsoka. Ahsoka is a version of Ashoka which means without sorrow. And even though I have depression and I got misgendered just last night, I feel without sorrow. I feel like I have a tiny sun instead of a heart. It has been forty minutes since the text arrived. And I have texted five people to tell them about my certificate and I have not done one bit of studying.

10/20/2022
No movement on the certificate.

10/21/2022
6:00 a.m.: It has moved states. It is now in my state.
1:30 p.m.: It has been dispatched, it was supposed to come on Monday or Tuesday but now it says it will be here in the next two hours. I'm so excited, but now a little bit nervous. It is going to be so hard to focus on my Zoom meeting.

2:50 p.m.: It arrived. I saw the postman and ran down the stairs. I requested my new birth certificate to have ducks and it doesn't have ducks, just eucalyptus leaves. Though I can't believe they folded my birth certificate in thirds to fit into a normal sized envelope. I was so excited that I burst into my sister's room yelling "Taylor Swift can wait, look." 3:00 p.m.: I have run downstairs to show my grandparents. They look so confused, but I don't care. I am just so happy to legally have a new name. They politely ask what Ahsoka means, I tell them it is an anagram of Ashoka which means without sorrow. The meaning was the final reason why I chose the name. I've had depression for so long and to me this name is a sign of my healing.

10/22/2022
I've already filed out the forms to change my name with my university. I'm working on the form to change it with my work, but the form isn't clear and that is so frustrating because I am impatient and want everyone to know my new name now.

11/17/2022
Work still hasn't processed my change of name form. I got a letter of promotion today, but it was in my birth name. I am so close to crying. Do they know how much that hurts? I email them back telling them that I will need a new letter of offer because it does not have my legal name on it.

11/23/2022
I got my new letter of offer with the right name on it.

12/09/2022
Today is my Rooster's, a term I have coined as a gender-neutral bucks/hens bachelor/bachelorette party. We have gone to Dream-World, where I have spent the day riding roller coasters. To leave DreamWorld you have to exit through the gift shop, which includes a Lego shop. As we are browsing, I spot an Ahsoka Tano key ring and show it to my sister. Who immediately says "I'll buy this for you." I'm not sure my sister knows how much this meant to me, because it isn't just Ahsoka Tano my favorite Star Wars character, it is my namesake. It is validation of my new name.

Ahsoka is added to my key ring before we get to the car and I show everyone when we get home.

12/12/2022

Today, I am marrying Will and I am marrying Will with my name.

Will is standing at the end of the aisle in his navy-blue suit and boutonniere that matches my bouquet. The sun is shining in through the floor-to-ceiling windows that look over the entire city. I am dressed in a white jumpsuit, with blue floral lace and blue shoes, but the outfit is really about the cape. Mum used over twelve meters of fabric to make this cape and spent close to sixty hours embroidering it. I'm worried I am going to trip over it, because I was told to walk down the aisle slowly (even though I just want to run up to Will). But the hours Mum spent on the cape is worth it because Will looks like he is watching a piece of art and I feel like I am invincible. And then I am standing next to Will and he is holding my hands and his hands are so warm and my sister is placing my cape so it sits just right.

When we first got engaged I was so worried I would have to get married with a name that wasn't mine, because I still didn't have a middle name. Then I was worried that the government wouldn't be able to process my name change in time.

But today I hear the love of my life say, "I call upon the persons here present that I, Will take you, Ari Ahsoka to be my lawfully wedded spouse." All I hear is that this man standing in front of me sees me fully. He sees my queerness, and not only does he accept it, he loves it. He sees my brain that can be a bit much, he sees my struggles, and my weaknesses, and my strengths, he just sees me.

After the ceremony, Will tells me very proudly that he told the celebrant to use spouse for both of us. He knew how important this was to me.

The only thing that made today better than marrying Will with my true name is the jam-filled doughnuts we had for dessert.

This new name is about people seeing the real me. The me I choose to be, the me that is learning to be comfortable in my own skin.

I've got a completely new name now and I am so excited to fill out government forms so that everyone knows my new name.

EGGPLANT

JESSICA WOODBURY

We meet at Danielle's house. I am nervous-excited but not so much that it's a vibration of anxiety, just a low hum of possibility. Even though we have all agreed to tonight in advance, a specific plan is not set. We will see how it goes.

This non-monogamy stuff is still new to me and I have not yet made any kind of official commitment to it. I am trying it out. A testing of the waters now several months long. Morgan, the one bringing us together tonight, is the evangelizing kind, perhaps a relic from his own religious upbringing, a full-blown relationship anarchist who is happy to answer my questions with long emails full of helpful links. There is a looseness to Morgan's life that I find slightly disorienting if not terrifying, but I like the effect he has on me. I am surprised by how much we have in common. He helps me feel brave. Once we rode rental bikes without helmets down the streets of Cambridge. I told him that would never happen again, too much risk for my faint heart. But tonight, going to meet Danielle for the first time feels just risky enough.

When I arrive, Morgan isn't there yet. I'd hoped he would be because I wanted to use my existing closeness to him to ease me into the night. Instead, it is just Danielle and me. She has dark, curly hair, a wide smile, and glasses. She is cute and just slightly bird-like. She is immediately welcoming, and I can tell within minutes we will get along. I understand why Morgan suggested this, why Danielle and I would be a fit. At least platonically, if nothing else.

We go into the kitchen where she is salting large chunks of eggplant. I do not say that I don't like eggplant, though in my head I am already strategizing how to get through the meal without giving any hint that I'm not enjoying it. Maybe if it was Eggplant Parm, doused in sauce and cheese, I wouldn't notice the bitterness, the tang it left in my mouth, the squishy texture. But no, this is a vegan meal, the eggplant is the center, the star of the show, and I will have to deal with it. I ask Danielle how I can help; she gets me started sauteing and we are deep in conversation by the time Morgan finally appears.

Strangely I get nervous again, even though he is supposed to be the familiar and comforting part of the night. My favorite part of my relationship with Morgan is after we have sex, when we lay together in bed and talk about the dates we've been on, who we slept with, what we liked about these other people. We love the details and ask each other lots of questions. We are alike this way and it is the happy camaraderie of these moments that I enjoy so much. I have heard Morgan talk about dates with other people, about sex with his other partners. But somehow seeing him in person with Danielle feels like it could be something different. He is closer to Danielle and they have been together longer. I wonder what she knows about him that I don't. I wonder how they will interact. Will I feel excluded? Will I feel like less? I try not to dwell for too long on these uncertainties.

They say hello then he pulls off a coat and removes his shoes. I look out the kitchen door and see the two of them embrace. A moment later, he is with me. I step back from my work at the stove. We greet each other, and his arms around me are warm even though his fingers and lips are cold. He has not given us identical hugs, has not given us equal portions of his affection. With Danielle he is more casual, it tells the story of their history and their comfort. His smile to me is bright but our touch shows our newness.

And it is all fine. It is just fine. I go back to the stove. Morgan finishes the salad. Danielle makes the dressing. It feels like we've done this before, gathered together to cook and eat like old friends rather than three people who might all end the night in bed together.

In the summer of 2015, not long before our evening together at Danielle's house, I was constantly on dating apps. I was looking for what everyone was looking for, I thought. I had seen a few people who admitted in their profile that they were non-monogamous or polyamorous and I didn't really understand what that meant. I avoided them.

I was a couple years deep into dating by then, I'd dived right in after a divorce and hadn't let up. My initial plan was to get remarried. I thought since I knew so clearly what I wanted that it would be simple to narrow down my options, that I would meet someone quickly. I went on a lot of dates but I almost never liked anyone enough to get into anything you'd call a relationship.

I was in my mid-thirties and not really swipe right material. I was divorced with two young children and rebuilding my life and career from basically nothing. There were better options than me. More than once someone unmatched me when they realized I had kids. More than one promising date didn't lead anywhere when I told them that I'd be offline half of each week while I had my kids at home, so I could give them my full attention. People got irritated by my schedule, by the fact that I generally only had time and energy to go out once a week, especially during the months when I worked two jobs to try and make ends meet.

The people I dated were frustrated with me but I was frustrated with them, too. Why did people demand so much of me when we'd just met each other? My life was intense and stressful. I was doing a lot of work at my actual job, work at home to parent my kids, and work in my own head to try and give myself some care, too. I didn't want a partner who would demand even more from me.

I was feeling this strain the first time I swiped right on a nonmonogamous person. He was a married cis man looking for fun and friendship and not a huge time commitment. He didn't sound like someone who only wanted something "casual" or a friend with benefits he would keep quiet. A part of me thought this was sketchy, that there was something predatory or shameful about it. But plenty of other profiles that looked good had led nowhere so I sent him a message.

We went on a few dates and it was refreshing. He thought I was funny and interesting and brave and he was happy to have our time together to be a break from everything weighing me down. He wasn't asking for no strings; he wanted an emotional connection. But he had a wife and kids to get back to so our time together was like a little vacation for both of us. Ultimately, we decided we weren't a fit, but I liked how easy and free it had been. I started to wonder if maybe there could be something worthwhile to this non-monogamy thing.

When the food is ready, Morgan and Danielle get all the dishes and silverware. They move easily, knowing where everything is. I sit in my seat so I don't get in anyone's way in the small kitchen. We dish up our plates and sit with our knees practically knocking at the little table. It is what they call a "dine-in kitchen," something city apartments always try to pass off as a feature but actually means you don't have any space for a real table.

I put plenty of salad on my plate. Then I dish up what seems like a politely acceptable portion of the eggplant dish, not so little that it would be noticeable, but not any more than necessary.

Conversation flows easily since Morgan is good at that. He asks Danielle about her other partner and how he is doing in school. He asks me how work is going and about the business trip I have coming up. I know he and Danielle have lots of friends and even some partners in common, but they keep me included in the conversation, never moving to the parts of their lives where I am the odd person out.

Through all of this I try to pay attention to how I feel about Danielle. I enjoy talking to her. I think maybe I would like to kiss her, but I am not sure yet. I struggle sometimes with women, still not feeling very confident about myself. It is a classic bisexual conundrum, with so many straight men around and so few queer women, it is much easier to date one than the other. I have less experience with women. Especially since I'd had a good seven-year head start dating only men and then a long stretch in a monogamous marriage with a man. Still, I knew they wouldn't mind—if anything they would understand. All three of us are bisexual, all familiar with the complications of dating across multiple genders.

More and more, especially after we open the bottle of wine, I feel like I want to kiss Danielle. The question is, would she kiss me? It is supposed to be a no-pressure night, just a vibe check. But surely it could be more than that if the vibes are good, couldn't it? I know now that I'll be disappointed if Danielle starts clearing the table, saying she'll be going to bed early, sending us out the door. Or maybe after dinner we'll sit around talking and it will get awkward and I'll realize that I am supposed to leave the two of them alone? No, I assure myself, Morgan is looking out for me. He already vouched for Danielle and her kindness. He is the most genial person I know and he loves making connections. I am positive this wasn't the first time he'd introduced two people thinking there could be a spark. He can handle it. I let myself relax a little.

I had never been a very jealous person. A decade earlier, my best friend ended our relationship when his new fiancée said she was uncomfortable with him spending time with me. Even if she was there with us. Even in a room full of people. My status as a single woman made me dangerous.

I was baffled by this. I was still Mormon then, in my last year of law school at BYU. I should have known the rules, that women and men weren't allowed to be friends. I didn't know any married men or women who had friends of the opposite gender. I didn't even know any unmarried people with friends of the opposite gender. But that friendship meant so much to me, it made me think there had to be another way, that what we shared was so important to the two of us that it would transcend the rules. I couldn't understand how he could end everything so quickly, so cruelly.

"You'll understand when you're married," more than one person told me.

But I didn't. True, my marriage was outside Mormonism, but I had learned that a similar set of rules still applied. If you were still friends with a former lover it was bound to get messy, everyone seemed to agree on this. Except me. My spouse spent time with his ex, they often studied together, spending hours without me. I didn't worry. I didn't feel like he was being taken from me. I couldn't imagine insisting he cut her out of his life. I thought often about that friendship, how I was now in a similar position to my ex-friend's now-wife and I felt none of what she felt.

I told Morgan this entire story on our first date, the two of us at a table in a pub for hours, nursing our drinks. It was a long date. The kind of date where you tell all of your big stories, where you can't stop talking because you keep finding more you have in common. The pub was no longer busy, in that slow period after the dinner crowd and before the late-night rush.

After I shared that story of lost friendship, Morgan was sympathetic. "That's really terrible," he said. "But I know how you feel. I didn't feel the way everyone said I was supposed to feel. I want a lot of things from life, I want a lot of people in my life, but I don't want to limit anyone else. I have a full life and part of why it's full is that the people in it have their own big, full lives, too."

The server came over to our table for the first time in a long time. She could see that we weren't ready to go and asked if we wanted dessert. Morgan said yes. And I did, too.

At Danielle's, a surprise. So far, the night has been unusually unsurprising. It is a strange and new situation, meeting one of my partner's other partners, and more than that, knowing that we would both be feeling each other out, wondering if we might have our own chemistry together. And yet it hasn't been surprising at all. Instead it has been comfortable and inviting.

The surprise is not Danielle; it is the eggplant. It is delicious. I admit to the table that I'd had my qualms, that I'd kept my mouth shut not wanting to make a fuss, determined to be a good guest. Danielle apologizes and I don't let her finish.

"No," I insist. "No apologies. I thought I hated eggplant and tonight I've learned that I don't. This is a very exciting night for me. I have a new person I like and a new food I like."

I take another helping. I'd been trying to tell myself that I wasn't all that hungry, that the salad would be plenty, that I would make it work. But now that I don't have the same restriction, I am ravenous. I want more. More of everything. I load my plate. Morgan tops off my wine glass.

We talk about the foods we don't like. I tell them how embarrassed I get about my picky eating, which feels nonexistent in my normal life when I control everything, but then starts to feel very large when someone suggests a seafood restaurant for a first date since I don't care for fish.

"You shouldn't feel bad about it," Danielle says. "You like what you like."

"I know you're right. But some people act like it's childish, like if I was a real adult, I would have figured out how to make myself like fish."

"Well, Danielle figured out how to make you like eggplant," Morgan notes.

We laugh. It's comfortable. I like Danielle, even if I never get to kiss her, tonight will still be a win. I have found another person that I like, a person who understands nonmonogamy and queerness when most people in my life are straight and married.

After I started seeing Morgan and imagining a life outside of the monogamy I'd always known, I started thinking about something else that seemed, at first, to be the exact opposite: living alone.

This idea didn't come from Morgan, who lived in a co-op with so many other people that even the thought of it exhausted me. There was even a small child I'd seen toddling around, and the idea of acting as an occasional substitute parent to any children other than my own was overwhelming.

In the weeks of limbo after separation but before divorce, the kids stayed in our apartment and I traded off time being home with them. When I wasn't there, I was in a studio sublet in another part of Boston. It was dark and uninviting, barely functional, the smallest kitchen I'd ever had in the many apartments I'd lived in. But when I was there that room was just mine. I had spent the last several years hardly ever away from my small children, working only sporadically, orbiting my whole life around my spouse's demanding career and my children's constant needs. When I first got to that little room, I could barely comprehend how quiet it was.

At first, I spent as little time in the room as possible. I wandered through the city, walking through my new neighborhood, riding the bus and the T to places I rarely got to go. I put in earbuds and listened to music, the songs still so familiar even though I realized I hadn't listened to them in years. I had forgotten what it was like to be alone. It was wonderful.

After I left that room behind, after the divorce, when my children were at their father's house, when my apartment was empty, when I was done with work and no one had any demands on my time, these were often the moments when I was happiest. They were also the times when I could ask myself if I still wanted what I'd always thought I wanted. Ten years earlier, even after my break from the Mormon Church and after recognizing my own queerness, I'd still thought I wanted to marry a man and have children. With the benefit of time and distance I could see that I hadn't wanted those things the way I thought I did. The last thing I'd wanted then was to be alone. To be alone was to fail, to be unwanted.

Now being alone was freedom. I started to imagine a life for myself that didn't have to be based on a predictable, well-worn model, but rather one that came from only myself without the distraction of what I *should* be.

Sometimes the quiet of my apartment after the kids left was bracing, a kind of whiplash after running around feeding and dressing and caring for two small children. Sometimes I missed having a person with me, someone else who cooked dinner or picked out the movie. But I treasured even more the times when I could cook whatever I wanted and pick the movie that I was in the mood for, without worrying about catering to anyone else's tastes. In relationships I tended to pull back, please, defer. I struggled to ask for what I wanted. As long as I had bandwidth and energy, I prioritized my partner's happiness.

I was starting to realize that non-monogamy was about wanting more in all kinds of ways. It was having more partners, having more ways to be. It also meant having more for myself outside of those partners, creating relationships where I could carve out my own space, deciding just how much of myself I wanted to give without a sense of obligation. There was more than one way to be. There didn't have to be a gulf between me when I was single and me when I wasn't. I could bring partners in and out of my life as I wanted to, as it made sense. I could have time to myself without feeling guilty. I could spend an evening alone without wondering or worrying what my partner was up to.

More than that, I could build a life without waiting for the right person or people to come along. There was a menu with many new things to try.

Before the kissing starts, I tease Morgan about the crowded house he lives in. We have moved out of the kitchen, taking our wine glasses with us, finishing off the bottle. Danielle and I sit on a loveseat, Morgan across from us.

Being in the city is getting to me, I admit. I dream of having no shared walls, no overheard conversations, no strange thumps from upstairs.

"I would love more space," Danielle says. "But I like the idea of having all my people all together. A little queer commune apartment building."

I say, "Have you ever seen *Big Love?*" I am embarrassed to say this, it is already a passe reference, off the air for years.

"No," Morgan says. "You watched it for the Mormon stuff?"

"I avoided it for a long time because of the Mormon stuff." I don't share all my complicated reasons, I know that here on the East Coast the religion I grew up in is foreign, a punchline more than a recognized culture or set of doctrines. I know that my little soapbox about Mormon representation in the media is not what I want at this moment. "But anyway, in the show there are these three houses on a regular suburban street. And this one family, with these three partnerships, is divided up among these three houses, all next door to each other. Each house is on its own, and the woman inside it runs it herself, has her own furniture and her own decorations. From the outside it just looks like three regular houses. But in back, there are no fences. So you have your own house, but you can also go freely into one of the other houses. I've been thinking about that a lot."

"But then you'd have to live in the suburbs," Morgan says.

The conversation pauses, it is slowing down as we feel the evening shift. There is the slight spark of electricity in the air between us all.

Before my thoughts come to a stuttering stop and my body takes over, I let myself appreciate the night. It is something new, I keep finding more new somethings ever since I met Morgan. I say I am just trying non-monogamy out, just seeing how it goes, but the truth I haven't yet admitted to anyone is how comfortable it makes me, even though it has only been a few months. The twist in my stomach as I brush Danielle's arm, the softness of her skin, the glow in the room, it feels like an invitation. Not just for this night but for a whole world. A world that I can build, full of love and possibility.

LEFT OF CENTRE

SHERRIE GAVIN

"Oh! You're left-handed!" I whispered to the woman in the dressing room of the temple, as if I had just discovered the most phenomenal thing in the world. She looked at me strangely. After all, she was writing names on the prayer roll list. "It's just …" I stumbled. Then, quickly trying to recover, "My daughters are both left-handed, and my husband and I are right-handed, and my father was left-handed, but he's dead …" This was not getting better. I was sounding weirder by the millisecond. "Is there anything I can do to support my daughters that I might not know?"

There. I said it. Only that is not what I really wanted to ask. I could never, ever ask anyone what I really wanted to know: Do I look like a mother?

Really?

Like a woman? A normal woman? An average woman?

I was born with Mayer-Rokitansky-Küster-Hauser, commonly called MRKH. In MRKH, genetic females are born without a uterus and without a vagina. Many only have a single kidney, some only have one ovary, some have an ovary and a testicle, some are deaf, and many others have a long list of other issues that are too numerous to detail.

This condition is discovered usually because the individual—who otherwise looks female—does not menstruate at puberty, or ever. Or, when a young teen tries to have sex, but can't. The lack of a vagina makes typical intercourse … atypical. When this is discovered, a chromosome test is completed, and then ultrasounds and even exploratory surgery.

I went through all of those things, and I hated every second. Most of the time, I submitted to the extremely invasive procedures

195

because my mother so desperately wanted to have a daughter—a real daughter ... not the kind of daughter that the United Nations considered within the intersex spectrum. "At least you don't have androgen insensitivity syndrome," my general practitioner told me. "They don't have pubic hair, and we have to remove their testicles. But they are still female."

Not a word of that made sense to me, except for the shaving part, so I focused on that. I was not a fan of shaving my bikini line and underarm hair, so I thought those girls were lucky. As it was, I went to so many specialists and endured so many invasive exams in my teens that when I finally went to college, a counsellor diagnosed me as a sexual abuse survivor.

The leftie in the temple thoughtfully paused. Then, after dropping her slip of paper into the prayer roll box, she said, "Have someone who is left-handed teach them how to tie their shoes." Then, "The rest they will figure out." I thanked her and pondered. Do I really lack so much confidence about my parenting that I was asking strangers for random help?

If God gave me these daughters to parent, and a birth mother chose me over hundreds of others as the right woman to raise her girls, and the courts have declared me their mother ... who am I to think I am not enough?

During my MRKH diagnosis phase, I was called as the stake Laurel representative for a regional youth conference. I attended one or two meetings where the adults pretty much planned everything, so I did not know why a Priest or a Laurel representative from any stake was necessary at all. The conference consisted of three days of activities that were arranged and organized by the adult leaders. By the end, I found myself sitting on stage at the college campus where the conference had occurred. There were two final speakers that the adults had arranged, and the stake youth reps were to bear testimony on cue of this fabulous conference that we had "helped" to plan.

The two final speakers were a husband-and-wife team, and were, from memory, a temple president and his wife. Before that moment, the world still seemed like my oyster—school, mission, maybe even graduate school, and adventure! I could not wait to hear from BYU that I had been accepted and was counting down the seconds to my high school graduation. The conference itself was captivating. Sure, there were the typical dances at night, but the days offered choices to attend sessions on political activeness, preparing for a mission, applying your patriarchal blessing in your life, and so on. Sure, there were some "Mormon womanhood" classes, but as we had been prompted to choose what interested us, I skipped all of those.

I can only remember the opening lines of the temple president's wife: "The most important role any of you young women have is being a mother." Suddenly, I felt like all the hot, bright lights were focused on me, the female imposter. Being anywhere in the intersex spectrum makes fertility exceedingly difficult, if not impossible. By then, I knew I could never become pregnant. I might not even be able to have sex. I debated walking out and glanced to the stage exit closest to me. I thought about walking across the stage and leaving ... but where would I go? The women's restroom? The adults in my stake would follow me, shaking their fingers accusing me of the sin of being born within the intersex spectrum, and I would be forever known as the shameful, imposter girl from my stake. No one would "sign off" on my going to BYU. They would all know that I was a walking lie: the Laurel who could never be a mother.

A dull, high pitch seared through my head, but only I could hear it. It was the kind of searing, painful migraine that brought peace because I could no longer hear any of the words being uttered. There I sat, drowning out everything spoken from that moment on. And when it was my turn to bear testimony, I shook my head, causing the liberating closing prayer to come sooner.

I could never be a mother. I skipped the bishop's interview for BYU and went elsewhere—a small school where I could disappear into the background to go through vaginal construction treatments. But I did not disappear. Not to everyone, at least. The best guy ever noticed me. And when I tried to scare him away with my lack of female organs, he would not budge. Instead, because his brother was married to a woman from China, he said, "We should adopt from China, to match the rest of the family."

We did not end up adopting from China, but we did end up adopting two perfect, beautiful girls. It was the most blissful and terrifying moment when we heard our attorney congratulate us on the adoption. Being not quite perfectly female always made me feel like maybe God would let me adopt boys. I was not good enough to be a girl, much less be a mother, so … if I were to parent, well, it would be boys, right? Or an intersex child. I could parent like a rockstar with anyone but girls, I was sure.

Instead, God brought me girls. I was more surprised than anyone, but I didn't say anything. Because early in the process of adoption, I began to fret. Though it was years away, the idea of trying to teach my (Possibly? Hopefully?) daughters how to use a pad terrified me. Or how to use a tampon. Or what having a period felt like. Or … you know. Girl stuff like that. 'Cause I had *no clue*.

And my daughters were left-handed.

Did I really want to outsource this whole motherhood thing every time something about my daughters was different to me? Wow. That would be way more than just left-handedness. Even way more than MRKH. Much more.

No. I did not want to outsource motherhood. Motherhood was hard-earned for me, and I loved my daughters with my whole soul. So I began to Google. There are a lot of handy "how to left-handedly tie shoes" videos there! And I bought a children's book about tying shoes that focused on the laces, rather than which hands did what. I even began to teach myself how to tie my shoes opposite to the way I had been tying them for decades.

In the end, I ended up asking my daughters to mirror me tying my shoes. Which they did, and in turn, they learned to tie their shoes. It was not the easiest thing to do; we had to practice for a few weeks to get it right. But it was fun! And now they tie their shoes. Soon we'll be in tampon territory. But I am their mother, and it is my gift to be able to teach them about this next step. This next step is going to be fun, too. They are going to have a life that is very different, and better, than mine. And it won't be just because of the tampons. It is because I get to be their mother. And I am good at that.

HOME COMES QUIETLY

RAE McCAUSLAND

The old guard house, found a long way down a grassy overgrown road, is all boarded up, tarps over the windows, moss on the roof. The outhouse is covered in spiderwebs and peeling greenish paint. After a long, lovely summer day visiting Cal's mom at her new log cabin in Washington and celebrating Cal's older brother's birthday with his husband and friends, our first task this early morning is to dust off the webs and scrape off as much of the old paint as we can. Cal wields the broom, wearing the white and rainbow sweatshirt I brought with us from San Diego. With each loud stroke of the scraper, I release a little bit of the pent-up tension I've been holding in all week.

"You know," I finally say, "how sometimes you know you're over-reacting to something, even though you know you shouldn't be so scared or things shouldn't hurt so much, and all you can do is wait for your brain to stop throwing a fit?"

"Uh … are you saying you're still feeling like that?" Cal asks. The white sleeves of the sweatshirt are kind of floppy, especially when they're pushed up to Cal's elbows. I wasn't sure about how it looked on me, but on them, I think it's really cute.

"It's not quite as bad anymore." I keep scraping. It's satisfying, seeing the old paint peel off like curls of cold butter. "I think yesterday really helped me. Being around your family … everyone's so easygoing, it reminded me that I'll always be welcome there no matter what."

"Well, yeah!" Cal's voice is loud and expressive, but I can hear the relief under their exasperation. "There's no reason any of that would ever change just because I might try dating someone else. When I said I might want to try doing things like that with someone, I didn't ever mean I was setting out to replace you. The Rae place in my life isn't one anyone else can fill."

"I know. I know, but here's how I think it worked in my brain. I think … I spent so long feeling like the way I love you isn't allowed, because it wasn't a straight man and woman, or because I couldn't make it fit what I thought a relationship was supposed to be, or whatever. And when you said that maybe you could be more cuddly if I could give up on our relationship being romantic, it felt to my brain like … like saying that my feelings, that I can't help, are keeping me from being closer to you. Like just another variation of being told I need to get rid of some of my feelings, or learn to feel things in the right way, in order to really belong with you. That's all."

"Oh. But whether you have those feelings or not, and whether I'm cuddly or not, has no bearing on how much I love you."

The morning chilliness is wearing off even more quickly from all the scraping. I pause for a minute to rest my arms and take in what Cal is saying to me.

I pick up a few curls of old paint that strayed off the tarp and into the stringy grass. "I think it really helped that you acted the same as always even while I was freaking out. Making silly noises and doing stupid voices and stuff like usual. You just let me work through it."

"Good. I didn't really know what else to do, so …" Cal is done with the broom and joins me in scraping the paint. "I'm glad you seemed to bounce back pretty fast. Especially since I actually am talking to a guy on a dating app now."

"Oh." My heart feels a bit like it fell backwards after finally making it up a flight of stairs. I take a minute to just scrape vigorously and see if I can calm the kneejerk response.

"Do you want me to talk about it or not?" Cal asks tentatively.

"I mean, I don't want you to have to hide anything," I say slowly. Recentering myself feels like trying to push the wrong ends of two magnets together.

"His name is Will. We've been chatting a bit, he seems like he's okay with things being mostly cuddly if it turns out that way."

"He knows you're ace?"

"Yeah, it's in my profile. I guess he's heteroflexible."

"What's he look like?"

"He has long hair."

I laugh a little. "Oh, nice. Androgynous?"

"Kind of. You know, if you feel like exploring romantic or sexual things with someone, you might think about trying a dating app too. Some of them seem pretty queer friendly. Like, everyone recommended to me is some flavor of gay or trans and there are a lot of ace and aro-spectrum people too."

"Maybe." I try to keep my mind open. "I just have a really hard time imagining that I'd feel comfortable considering that kind of thing with anyone but you."

"I know. But even if you just want to make more friends, there's an option for that too."

"Yeah ..."

"Anyway, we don't have to keep talking about it if you don't want to."

"No, it's alright."

And it is, actually. The green July morning keeps growing warmer. Once the outhouse is stripped of most of its paint, there's still other work to do.

Back in San Diego, months later, I climb up the stairs of the townhouse we share with the landlady's two adult sons. Cal is in their room, and I come and plop down on the bed.

"I don't know what I'm doing," I groan dramatically.

"Uh oh, what?" Cal settles more comfortably on the bed with me.

"It's so weird, I normally feel totally oblivious to people's romantic cues, but tonight after it was time for me to go, we'd been watching *She-Ra* and I felt like the way Riley was looking at me, she was hoping I'd stay longer or kiss her goodbye or something. But then I thought, no, I was probably imagining it. But then she texted me after I got home to ask if I had any desire to kiss her!"

"Whoa. Well, do you?"

"I don't know ... I mean I'm curious, and I like her, but I don't know if that's the same thing as actually feeling like I want to kiss her in the same way like ... a person normally does in a romantic relationship. It's not like I'm in love with her at this point since we've only hung out a few times. But how do people even just do that? Like even if I think it might be nice, in the moment actually doing it feels impossible, like—really intimidating. And not because I feel like she'd pressure me or anything but … geez. People really do this all the time even on first dates. I can't imagine."

"Yeah … kissing is weird." Cal turns the light off and flops onto their back. Their second-story window is open to the mild San Diego night. Maybe in a little while we'll hear Milo the orange cat come back from his nightly wanderings, trilling to announce his return before jumping over the wooden gate. "Even when I had such a big crush on Michael, actually doing anything like that felt like … nope, when I actually tried it."

"Yeah. I feel really ace right now. It's like, I'm in my thirties and I know I've told Riley that I have next to no experience with anything like this, but it must be hard for her to wrap her brain around what it's like. I feel like I've been trying to go along with this dating thing like 'when in Rome' but that was my mistake with Sabrina too, and we know how that turned out. It's been a while since I realized that I just approach relationships in a completely different way than most people. The timeline is different. The way things develop is just different. I don't want to accidentally hurt her by trying something and have her read feelings into it that aren't the same as hers."

We're both lying there in the dark, on piles of pillows and a rumpled duvet. There's the whoosh of cars from the next street over. Cal makes a pensive noise. "I kind of realized that I don't like it when people feel like … entitled to my space or to acting close to me when we've only just met, or even have hung out several times. It takes a lot for me to let someone feel like they have a claim on my attention or my personal bubble. Like just because we both find each other attractive … when I met up with Will I was really feeling like, excuse you, you're in my space. And it wasn't even like he was being pushy or anything, it was just the expectation of how people typically behave on a date."

"Yeah. So it would probably take a long time for that to develop, huh?"

"I think if the infatuation isn't there from the beginning, it's really unlikely that anything physical will happen. My whole discomfort with people being in my space is just too strong."

The air is the perfect temperature. After the initial little twinge at being reminded that Cal will probably never be as into cuddling as I am, I feel a rush of happiness, but it's not the intense relief I expected from hearing that Cal is basically done with trying to date other people. It's calm, like the forest air around the guard house back in July. Like the cool swirl of mud and water around my calves as I mucked out the old reservoir with a shovel, tossing globs of mud, pinecones, and other debris over the low cement wall. Things start to feel clearer, to flow again.

It's strange to realize that from the outside, our relationship, our identities, look confusing and indistinct. My cautious forays into the dating world have felt so much more precarious than my steps through the quicksand-like mud of that reservoir, the floor shifting under my feet. Still, in stirring up that muck, something bright had floated to the surface. Natural specks of mica, golden glitter swirling wherever the sun-speckled water was disturbed.

I say, "This whole thing is making me realize that the main reason I don't feel constantly abnormal or like some alien on a foreign planet is because I don't really engage with dating culture most of the time. It's *so* nice that I don't have to if I don't want to."

"Yeah."

"I don't have to second guess or explain all the meanings behind my actions with you. I don't have to worry about you reading things into how I respond that I didn't mean. It's so nice!"

"It is."

"Why don't more people live like this? It's so much easier. But I guess they just operate differently. And we do have the advantage of knowing each other and growing up together for more than a decade."

"Yeah, and it wasn't always easy. We had a lot of tough times."

"Yeah. It took a while to really understand each other. But now ..."

In the other room, one of the boys starts singing a toneless off-key repetitive song.

"Ah, the nightly concert." Cal gives a longsuffering sigh.

We laugh a little. We lay in the dark, quietly knowing each other in a way that no one else in the whole world does, a way that requires no physical touch at all. It's a holy space built up of all our history, but not constricted by it, not smothered by it. In this moment, I don't know where we'll be this time next year, or what labels we'll use to define our relationship—best friends, queerplatonic partners, or something else. But for the moment I feel completely relaxed and at ease, confident in the fact that this is home. It is completely and uniquely ours; there is nothing else like it anywhere.

SPRING 1

STACEY HARKEY

When I came out to my bishop, his jaw hit the floor. I had previously been teaching stake institute and currently had a handful of callings in the ward.

He looked at me stunned and whispered, "but how … you're so *good*."

I spent a large portion of my life trying to "fix" myself. I put so much energy into trying to mend what I thought was a "broken me."

I found myself on my knees, praying and begging to know how to move forward … and that beautiful experience helped me realize I'm not broken. I'm exactly who I need to be.

That's been one of the most validating aspects of coming out and dating. I didn't realize how sad I was in the closet until I experienced the joy of being myself.

A little over a year ago when I was overwhelmed by the unbearable pressure of grappling with my sexuality and all the joys that came with it—the intense loneliness, immense cognitive dissonance, etc.—I would drive down a country road, usually late at night, crank "Spring 1" by Max Richter, and beg and plead with any higher power willing to listen to fix this dreadfully painful part of my life. I would take deep breaths and attempt to summon the strength needed to not implode.

Right at this moment, I'm driving down the same road and "Spring 1" by Max Richter is blasting away. I just left my boyfriend's house where he looked me in my eyes and told me how thankful he was for me and I'm heading home to a houseful of incredibly supportive friends.

I'm overcome with emotion as I realize: someone heard my desperate pleas.

I look back at how painfully wrong it was versus how perfectly right it is now. I feel whole and complete in a way I never knew I could.

I feel right.

I feel closer to myself and my God like never before.

Sometimes I have to stop what I'm doing and just thank God because of the overwhelming joy and peace I feel.

CLAIMING QUEERNESS

VANESSA BENNETT

"We stan the gays in this household," I told my little sister. It was Thanksgiving. My husband and I were visiting my parents. The air was rich with the scent of turkey and vegetables.

I don't remember the exact context of it. But I remember her eyes going a little wide. She was barely fourteen. A pimply, gangly wisp of a thing.

Possibly the words had never been spoken aloud in that house before. *We stan the gays.* Or, more precisely: *if you are queer, I am a safe person.*

My older sister, Sophia, and I had been texting about it for months. We're both happily, proudly queer. I am nonbinary and some degree of asexual. She is bisexual. But we're … not out. Not really.

I came out on Facebook in a messy bout of post-2016 election grief at the ripe old age of seventeen. I have mentioned being queer on family-facing social media exactly once since. I'm willing to talk about my own queerness—clearly—just not where my parents, grandparents, and other extended family members can see.

Sophia came out to me in 2015, because I asked if she was bi. That may be the only time she's come out to anyone.

I am terrible at noticing other queer people unless they explicitly tell me. Sophia's gaydar is excellent. And it had been pinging about our little sister. We talked about it constantly.

How do we let her know we're *queer without forcing her into coming out? How can we point her towards good queer representation in TV shows and books? How do we tell her she's not the only queer kid in this very Mormon family?*

In the end, it was simple: *we stan the gays*, in which the *we* meant "Sophia and me, and hopefully you too."

The next year, I was back at my parents' house for Christmas. Opened presents were strewn across the living room. Mom was setting out chips and dip, the traditional Bennett holiday lunch.

My little sister walked over to me, hesitant. "Can we talk? In my room?" She gestured upstairs.

"Sure."

She led. I followed.

Her room was tidier than I remembered. Books were neatly lined up on three different bookcases. Her backpack sat in the corner. The hideous pink walls, best described as Barbie camouflage, were covered with anime-style illustrations of characters for the stories she wrote with friends. And also hand drawn pride flags.

She closed the door behind us. I plopped down on her bed.

"So," I said, "what's up?"

She took a deep breath. "I wanted to let you know that I'm gendervoid and asexual."

I nodded. "Cool. I'm here for you."

I was trying to seem nonchalant. I don't know if I succeeded. Nobody had ever chosen me to be the safe adult before. This felt radiant. Like a burst of light breaking through cloud cover. Pure light, pure joy, the truth of another person revealed to view, made extra special because it was happening here. At home. Three siblings, years apart, discovering our queerness the same way church leaders suggested revelation happened: slowly, steadily, until one day a breakthrough happened and the world never seemed the same.

"Do you think I should tell Mom?"

I thought about it for a moment. "Probably not. She didn't take it well when I did."

My sibling froze. "What do you mean?"

"Well, when I came out five years ago, she asked me how I could be nonbinary when the Family Proclamation says we're created male and female. She's been better over the past few years, but I haven't been at home. And I pass as a straight woman. Especially after marrying Gavin."

"You're nonbinary?"

"Yeah. I've mentioned it before. Do you not remember?"

They shook their head. "I had no idea."

"Oh. Well. I am. I wrote an essay about it in a book that's coming out next year. And I'm ace, too." I picked up my phone. "Can I text Sophia and ask her to come up? She's also queer, but she can tell you the details."

My sibling sank into a nearby chair. "Sure?"

I texted Sophia something short and sweet. *We were right! They're queer too!*

A minute later, Sophia bounded up the stairs and knocked on the door. I let her in.

"You're queer?" Our younger sibling asked as soon as the door is closed again.

"Yeah. I'm bi." Sophia shot me a hard look, as if to say, *you brought me upstairs for this?*

"I'm gendervoid and asexual."

I piped up. "What do you want us to call you?"

They said they don't feel any attachment to their birth name. "My friends call me Cryptid."

Sophia and I exchanged a confused glance. We wanted to be supportive. Our job was to be supportive. We knew the stats about accepting adults reducing the risk of queer teen suicide. We had not thought about the sorts of names a pack of queer teenagers would pick for themselves. "Cryptid?"

I opened the contacts app in my phone and showed Cryptid as I changed their name. They beamed at me afterwards, delighted, but a little shocked.

"I'll text my friends," they said, "and let them know it went well. And that my sister is actually my sibling. And that my other sister is bi."

"Sounds good," I said.

Sophia and I filed out of the room. Our work was done for the moment. Cryptid knew we loved them and that they're not alone.

"You know," I told Sophia, "in a family as big as ours, there's no way we're the only queer kids."

"I just hope they have a support system."

"Yeah."

I can't be certain, but I suspect we were thinking the same thing: *we have to let our cousins know we're affirming.*

I wasn't surprised at all when, a little over a year later, I got a text from Sophia.

Cousin Jack just changed his Pokemon Go avatar to a girl. I don't want to make any assumptions, but ...

A SACRAMENT OF QUEERS

LAVVYNDER ROSE

I have picked the perfect Pinot Noir to pair with my dinner. Everything is just as I like it: the tofu crisp on the outside soft and spongy inside. The sauce wafts an overwhelm of garlic—perhaps a chef's nightmare: over-seasoned, ruined, unpalatable. *Delicious.*

I remember, at twenty-two, when I purchased that first bottle of wine from the liquor store and the fear that came with it. "What if someone saw you!?" a past lover had said.

The dog waits, patient, at the edge of the kitchen. I tempt her with my cooking—I'm a devil for keeping an innocent snack out of her reach. Her puppy eyes are irresistible, but her stomach is more fragile every day. I excessively tease her and she may love it; still, she'll get a cookie, catered to her tricky diet, after dinner.

I remember, at twenty-four, when I first brought my Daisy girl home and the disappointment of my family; the expectation that by now I'd be giving them grandkids.

Dinner is served and I remove my apron. My cropped tank reveals my tattooed tummy—where I place my hand, a gentle touch—it is warm, I am warm. My girlfriend sneaks up behind me "thank you for dinner," they say as they wrap their hands around me and gently squeeze my breasts. A small kiss on my cheek as I breathe deep their smell of sweat, earth, and love.

I remember, at eighteen, when I had confessed to Bishop Beck, "I touched her breasts ..." with a fire of embarrassment in my chest.

We sit across from one another; they reach across our small thrift-store table and take my hands in their own. I smile at the sight—my purple chipped fingernails, theirs a much fresher coat of pink. I breathe a silent prayer, not to God, but to them: the peace in their gold-flaked sea-foam eyes, the quiet smile on their lips, their imper-fect tapestry of freckled skin, the *S O F T* inked into their left hand.

I remember, at age six, as my sisters painted their nails I had asked, "Can I paint mine too?" but I received a parental reprimand. "Let's pick something else that boys can do."

I find no need to grasp at crumbled bread in a tray.

I no longer stop to count the sins—I no longer see them this way.

The wine is delicious.

My girlfriend is so fucking hot.

My body is mine to adorn and decorate.

A gender: mine to discover, change, create.

No need to pray in fear.

We laugh over our pasta as the night blurs between sips. Our shared gaze, divine. I pull their hands in and kiss them. "My love," as I rub their fingers between mine and turn my lips to a sly smile. "How about some dessert?"

I'm home. We're home.

JOY IS THE MOST BEAUTIFUL FEELING

ANDI YBARRA

The air was both warm and cool. It gets that way this time of year at Yellowstone, when it's just on the edge between summer and fall. You put the hood of your hoodie on or take the whole thing off entirely based on if you're in the shade or not.

Where I was sitting on the porch of the photography building was in the shade. I pushed my hands deep into my hoodie pouch.

Any minute now. Any minute she would erupt. I leaned forward, excitement gathering in my stomach as I waited.

Old Faithful and I could probably have been considered old friends at this point. Every summer growing up my grandparents would take me and my siblings through the park. I'd been to the park twelve different times before this one. This time though, the thirteenth visit, was different from those summer trips.

I was here to stay for three months with a job. As a kid I'd seen the people who worked there as if they were almost mystical beings, and now I was one! My mornings were foggy-breathed walks to work and most of my free time was out on the trails. I'd also brought my partner with me, something I couldn't have imagined in my childhood daydreams.

I couldn't have guessed at twelve that my stay here would have included a partner. I couldn't imagine anyone who would have wanted to live in the middle of nowhere for three months! My partner, Tim, was a better partner than I could have imagined for myself.

It was just a few weeks after he'd started testosterone shots when we'd come to the park. We could tell because people still looked at us like we might be sisters, which led to some weird conversations. Usually though, we went around holding hands, feeling brave when someone would send a nasty look our way.

Today, he was stuck behind a cafe counter. Which was why I wasn't able to just steal the beanie right from his head when it was cold.

I had made my way to this specific spot because it was a Sunday afternoon. I'd moved into the park right after being told I was too queer to be Mormon anymore. I wanted to give the time that was usually spent in beige, burlap lined chapels to this sanctuary of pine trees.

And so I kicked at the little pieces of gravel that had stuck themselves between planks of the porch while I waited for service to begin.

When small spurts of water started to shoot in the air I couldn't help but smile with fondness at the gasp of wonder from everyone. Even I shifted to the very edge of my seat, stopped rocking, and watched more intensely even though I knew it may still be another thirty minutes before it would reach its full height.

When we visited with my grandparents we always sat at the front and dangled our legs off the edge of the platform, kicking the air with excitement. Other times I'd watched it from the balcony on the second floor of the inn, or from the trail. But never from the spot I was sitting at right now, and it felt extra special to be here.

When Old Faithful finally shot into the sky, I felt the small piece of my soul that lived with it take off as well. The kid who had first come into the park over a decade ago reappeared as I watched the steam turn into an eyelet lace pattern in the cool mountain air.

The way I felt in that moment was the most beautiful feeling. It was like flying and dancing in the mist. It felt like finding a part of me that had gone missing in the years I'd spent pretending to be someone else.

It felt like joy!

As a teenager I had been told so many times that the path to joy was straight and narrow; there was a strict list of things I could do to reach that joy. I was also taught that anyone who didn't follow that narrow path to feel joy wasn't *really* feeling joy, instead it was a copycat of the real thing.

When I'd taken the first steps off that path a few months before I had spent almost every moment of my days waiting for that other shoe to drop. Expecting everything to suddenly be horrible, and let me tell you, what a godawful way to live.

However, even though I was waiting for the trapdoor to hell to open beneath my feet, I *was* happy.

I was happily in love with my trans fiancé.

I was happily ordering my pumpkin spice lattes.

I was happily trying alcohol at elevations no one should ever drink at because next thing you know you're face down in a pile of snow while you and your friends nearly sobbed with laughter at the silliness of the situation.

I felt like I was radiant with joy as the tower of water started to retreat back into the earth. The wind shifted and I got some mist on my face. I closed my eyes, tilted my head up and just let myself sit in the moment. It felt like the earth itself was holding my face to press a soft maternal kiss to my forehead.

When I got up from that porch after the crowds had dissipated, I was now sure of something. That my life would be framed in two pieces; before the moment on the photography building porch and after it.

And in my pocket, you would find, along with a small rock I'd picked up earlier, the first glowing shred of hope and healing that had been born of the joy I felt that chilly but sunny afternoon.

THE ANSWER TO A QUESTION NOT ASKED

ALMA FRANCES PELLETT

Four years ago, life was in a good place. I was coping well with my gender dysphoria, had a good job, and nothing big to complain about with my spouse or children. The pandemic brought the gift of working from home, communication handled through video call and email. The children's home schooling was a challenge but had turned into a blessing. My coping mechanism of wearing skirts when at home was able to move to full time, as it neither affected my work nor was it noticeable on video calls.

But there are times when life changes dramatically. If you're lucky, you're given a choice in the matter.

Part of the teachings of the Church of Jesus Christ of Latter-day Saints is "personal revelation." This is balanced against the hierarchical authority of the church. It can leave some things open for "local adjustment" or "individual adaptation" (thank you, Proclamation on the Family). Ideally, there is no conflict, but it can happen, and how that is handled can vary widely with which revelations are in conflict and the personal feelings of the people and leaders involved.

Much of the time, personal revelation translates to simple answers to prayer. The little inspirations to go one way or another, help making the right choice in life situations, the simple nudge of memory of where you left your car keys. But sometimes God can be a lot more direct and insistent. I've had four of these that I can recall, each one vitally important to my life at the time, so I've learned that God can be insistent to the point of annoyance when They want to be, and that when you get something so explicit you need to just drop everything and do.

The most recent for me was loud and clear: it was time for me to transition, socially and medically changing life to live as a woman.

That wasn't in my plans. It would add extra stress to my family at a time when my spouse was already working on moving into her own place. My health insurance wouldn't cover a single bit of it. I truly enjoyed going to the temple, even being on the "wrong," gender segregated side. I'd spent almost ten years working for the church in the Church History department, where being able to go to the temple was required to keep employment. My gender dysphoria was being managed well through counseling and simply knowing it was real. Why would I want to upend my life, adding even more trouble by being openly transgender in a church and place that can be very transphobic?

Could I have pushed back? Absolutely. But one thing I've learned is that, for me, God doesn't take no for an answer. They can be obstinate, even when the direction seems impossible to accomplish.

So I did one of the things I typically do when having a big question I don't understand as well as I'd like: I went to the temple. I was painfully aware of it possibly being my last time as I went through the motions of the session, a deep feeling of longing to join my sisters overwhelming anything else I might have gotten from the experience.

As I was admitted into the Celestial Room, all my worries and anxieties melted away. I took a deep breath, walking slowly through the room and immersing myself in the feelings of love, peace, and holiness I'd found throughout my years of visiting different temples. I let myself wander a little to admire the craftsmanship of the room and its furnishings, my favorites being the complicated glass art of the windows and the fine joinery of the few drawers in tables and chests that are rarely, if ever, used. The work put into all of it is always exquisite while often being overlooked, and I like to appreciate well done craft, in all its forms.

Visitors to the Celestial Room, in every temple, come in many kinds. Some hurry to get through and back to whatever other things they have in life. Some sit quietly alone, hoping for some comfort for their grief or answers to help ease their distress. Some treat it as a moment to share with close friends and family, enjoying the feeling of togetherness they hope will be repeated in the afterlife. Some simply spend it in quiet communion with their God. I've been all of those over the years.

I finally found a seat to myself in a wingback chair set against a wall on one side of the room. It wasn't terribly comfortable, as the seating in the room never gets broken in through loving use, but it was a good place to be on my own and meditate and pray on what had brought me to the temple. I took a deep, cleansing breath, bowed my head and closed my eyes and began to pray.

"I know you've asked this of me," I whispered to myself, "making this jump to actually transitioning after so many years just knowing who I am."

"I know I will continue to lose so many things my life has been built with, things I thought were absolutely stable in my life. But …" I had to take another deep breath. I could feel a tear building and was suddenly afraid to say what I have come here to say.

But I don't know how.

And that was really the crux of it all. Giving up family, work, friends, safety, community, all of it was fairly easy. But being actually at the threshold, stepping into the dark and mysterious unknown, I was terrified.

A few tears managed to escape with a ragged breath. I took another moment to compose myself.

"I will trust in thy plan for me."

I felt a wave of love deep into my soul. My tears changed from fear to relief. It was still dark and unknown ahead, but it would be ok. I am a daughter of Heavenly Parents. I gathered myself together and made my way out of the temple with my reaffirmed confidence, likely never to return.

Changing jobs was the most straightforward, but the most stressful. Coming out to my coworkers was the easy part, done when I had the new job in hand and during the two-week notice I felt they deserved. I went one at a time through those who have worked closely with me, then to the larger team on my last day. Not a one of the men I had worked with had much more reaction than being sorry to see me go, not even a single one asked what name I was thinking of.

Purchasing new garments, the special underwear we commit to wearing through our lives, was surprisingly easy. Get one, see how it fits and feels, either try again or get more. Tops were very little problem, the styles made for women of various bust sizes. Bottoms I ended up deciding to stick with the men's version, as my hips simply did not fit the expected shape of the women's version and had extra layers to hold things in place.

For church, I had a plan. I would meet with my bishop, hand in my temple recommend (not wanting to put them through the trouble of deciding what to do about me), explain the restrictions I'd placed on myself (no bathroom, no Relief Society 'til invited), and simply show up like any other week. That done, I dressed in what little I had, a poorly fitting black blouse and skirt, strengthening myself with my grandmother's red scarf and great-grandmother's rose brooch my mother had gifted me the Christmas before. The welcome from some and distaste and avoidance of others was clear in my ward.

The medical changes, such as hormone replacement therapy, were not difficult to learn about, but were difficult in figuring out how to get in conservative Utah. Endocrinologists and doctors willing to try were few. I finally ended up seeking an online service to get and monitor my hormone suppression and intake. Any surgeries would have to wait a full year after starting hormones.

Within the first few months I had noticeable breast growth. It was incredibly affirming, but also scary. Was my body doing it right? My primary care physician wasn't comfortable in her knowledge of transgender healthcare, but she could at least lend some knowledge in this area. Breast growth in a teen or expectant mother was routine and simple; in an over-forty transgender woman it simply wasn't in her experience. She kindly explained what was involved in doing a breast exam, brought me a gown to cover myself and allow the needed access, and left me to change.

I had no idea what to expect. I did my best to remain calm, stripped to the waist, put on the gown, and sat awkwardly on the exam table. The doctor smiled gently as she came back in, noticing my unease.

"Have you noticed any lumps, anything that I should look for," she asked while describing every step of what she was going to do when touching me.

I tried not to flinch too much as she examined each breast; new breast growth can be painful and sensitive. "I don't believe so," I answered, "but honestly I have no idea whatsoever what growing breasts *should* feel like."

She finished her examination. "Well, I don't feel anything odd, but we'll get you into a mammogram just to be sure."

It wasn't an experience I thought I'd need to have yet, especially with my smaller, still growing breasts, but I did it anyway. The technicians were kind and supportive throughout, commiserating at the pain and awkwardness and doing what they could to make me comfortable through this uncomfortable procedure. They even made a point of asking my pronouns, as my appearance certainly did not match the information on the medical records they'd been given.

The radiologist who looked at the x-rays and ultrasounds was brusque and to the point. "That's just growing breast tissue. Nothing to worry about."

And with that, I marked off one of many experiences that tend to be had by women and are completely new to me. That list continues to grow.

Clothing, makeup, hair, all of it I was unprepared for. I didn't want to do any of it wrong, my body was not shaped correctly (in my opinion) for women's clothing, my hair getting curlier and more unmanageable as it grew longer, makeup an overwhelming mass of options, products, and styles.

The hardest part? Patience. Puberty takes time, years, to adjust the body, even when you're older than usual. But through all the changes, I've held onto the comfort of knowing who I am, a daughter of Heavenly Parents, holding onto the outstretched hand of Jesus as we travel this new path.

The best part of it all? Gender Euphoria. It is the opposite of Gender Dysphoria, where a person feels unease about the mismatch between the gender they were assigned and their gender identity. I would describe it as "delicious to the taste and very desirable," and can't help but share each new aspect of my life that causes it. Trying on dresses in a women's clothing store, measuring my chest and finding them big enough to need a bra, getting my first piece of junk mail with my proper name on it, being complimented on my shoes (of all things), and most of all, finding people genuinely surprised to learn I am transgender. The list goes on and on, and I want to keep enjoying it forever, never taking for granted a single drop of goodness.

My journey continues, even though I consider my transition done. I am wholly a woman; the rest is details. I know I would be without any changes at all, but my transition was this journey of changing my attitude and some outward appearance, to be able to see myself in the mirror and enjoy the smile of the woman reflected back at me.

Despite all the difficulties in family, work, and church, life has become so much better than it was. I not only know who I am, but can show others the joy I have in expressing it. I can spend time with local LGBTQ support groups, helping others along their own paths. I can go out dancing, meeting new groups and trying new things, simply being just another woman out in the world. I can continue to navigate my own relationship with my God and my church. I can be the stay-at-home mom like the many others I'd held as examples since I was a child.

I can be me.

Forever grateful to have been given an answer to a question I never asked.

HOMECOMING

JACLYN FOSTER

About a year after I came out, my mother-in-law texted my wife to let her know the church was revamping their "Mormons and Gays" website and was seeking people to participate in focus groups. She asked if we would be interested, and we said yes. Kya, still closeted as bi and eggy as trans, attended the session for family and allies. The other sessions were segregated along binary gender lines: gay and bisexual men went to one group, and later that evening, lesbian and bisexual women had their own meeting.

I drove slowly along the Salt Lake City side streets, parallel parking hesitantly in front of the address I'd been given. I had been expecting an office building, but this looked like an expensive, historic home. I mounted the steps, knocked, and was let into the front room. I looked around, still unable to tell whether this was a full-time church building or whether someone was lending out their home for this. As some of the men filed out of what was either a dining room or a conference room, one of the women I waited with made friendly small talk with a man she recognized, apparently from North Star. We quietly entered the room and sat down around the table, and she blew out a long sigh. Apparently, their friendly conversation masked—at least on one side—a deep personal dislike, perhaps even a distrust of what he would have told the committee.

The facilitator had us go around the table, introducing ourselves. There were six of us, all celibate or in opposite-sex marriages. One was a teenager who had to produce her parents' signatures on a special waiver. Introductions done, the facilitator began recording and we started reviewing copies of different sections of the proposed site. We fell into a rhythm of reading and annotating, discussing, then reading again. We were critical. "We all know the doctrine, and all the straight members know the doctrine," we explained. "These feel so eager to hammer it home and it's just more painful. It feels like you think we don't understand. We do understand. We need other members to understand *us*."

The facilitator was professional, understanding. It was the first time I'd discussed this topic with a representative from the church who didn't get defensive, who seemed to truly listen. About an hour into the evening, I looked around the table, realizing something special was happening. I had been out for nearly a year, but this was the first time I had ever been in a group of exclusively queer women, my first time being extensively acknowledged as a queer woman. I had procrastinated going to the Understanding Sexuality, Gender, and Allyship (USGA) meetings, worried that my presence as a married mom would somehow be unwelcome, drastically overestimating the uniqueness of that scenario at BYU of all places. The irony of my first in-person queer meeting being facilitated by the LDS Church headquarters was not lost on me. The feeling was subtle. Something I'd never felt before. Something that filled me with a warmth and a witness I had exactly felt before. Something I had waited my whole life to feel.

It was the feeling of community.

A few months later, the revamped Mormon and Gay website was released. They left the preachy parts in.

————————

"A few of us are going up to Rexburg," Daniel texted. "Ellie has cancer and hasn't been to church because of it, and the Relief Society hasn't been by to help at all. So Nathan suggested we all get an Airbnb and clean their apartment."

I immediately agreed—not only for the service and friendship but because, frankly, I would have agreed to any excuse to be out of town for a weekend. Kya, Zoë, and I drove up in one car, and I wondered whether a toddler would defeat the purpose of going over to clean. Everyone else carpooled in Daniel's car. Zoë, fortunately, proved to be easily entertained, and I deep-cleaned the bathroom while Daniel handled the kitchen. Kya's fastidiousness with folding laundry came in handy.

Apartment cleaned, we ordered Panda Express and went over to the larger Airbnb to eat. I remember being so tired, but nobody seemed to want to go to bed. We talked, and laughed, and stayed up until three in the morning. Staggering out the door before our checkout time, I tried not to be too grouchy when the McDonald's drive-through in Rexburg, Idaho, had a limited menu on Sunday mornings. The drive home felt longer than the drive up.

It was, I would write later, the best church I'd had in years.

––––––––

Kya's hand gripped mine tightly as we walked through the empty parking garage. "You look pretty," I offered. Her short black wedges—thrifted from D.I.—clacked on the ground. She had chosen a chambray jumpsuit that no longer fit me, and her purple eyeshadow and lipstick brought her short hair from a man's haircut to a feminine pixie.

She nodded and kept walking as we entered the street, continuing on the short block towards the comedy club. We presented our tickets and walked through the doors. Immediately to our left sat Becca and Emily (in retrospect I think we crashed one of their early dates). I shoved Kya in beside them, placing myself protectively between her and any strangers who might sit at the next table.

She slowly relaxed as she looked out over the murmuring audience. "That's a lot of flannel," she joked, and I agreed in a voice that said *I told you so. I told you a Cameron Esposito show would be a great place to go out en femme.*

A local comedian opened with some jokes about being gay in Utah, and then Cameron took the stage. Apparently, she hadn't originally been slated to come to Salt Lake—she'd been hired for a private show in Park City, and she poked gentle fun at the decision to hire her for an audience that turned out to be deeply uncomfortable with strap-on jokes. But she had insisted, she said, on doing one night in Salt Lake. She had insisted on visiting the Utah Pride Center during the afternoon, had insisted on sending free show tickets to Queer Meals volunteers.

As the show went on, it became obvious why she'd insisted. She talked about the vulnerability of injuring herself on tour in the South and having the conversation in the ambulance turn to her job, half-naked, when she didn't know if the paramedics were queer-friendly. She had us all roaring with laughter. She talked about a different show in Tennessee, getting heatstroke performing at an outdoor festival. The paramedic that time had been a lesbian, with a rat tail so long it could tuck into her belt. She had ribbed Cameron about performing in a leather jacket when it was 100°. "I can't take it off," Cameron remonstrated, "It's part of my gender." A little un-named piece of me clicked into place.

Cameron abruptly stopped. "Are those … Mike's Hard Lemon-ades?" she asked a table in the front row. "I feel like I've time-traveled back to the '90s. It's like seeing a Furby on the table. I didn't know anyone still drank those."

"We're babies," one of the women explained.

"How old?"

"Twenty-five."

"Ah, yes. Mere infants!"

They bantered some more, and the women clarified that they were new to drinking alcohol, as they had recently become engaged and left the Mormon Church as a result.

Cameron's tone shifted, and she began to talk about what it was like to grow up queer and Catholic. It was funny, of course, and pol-ished—she was no stranger to doing bits about this topic—but also clearly not a planned part of her set, at least not at this juncture. *I see you*, she seemed to say. *I've been there too.* "And even though I'm not religious anymore, every December Celine Dion comes on the radio and I think to myself, should I … go to church?" *You never quite lose that estrangement from your first community, but you have one here too.*

After the show, Cameron hung back to take pictures with the audience. I had always scoffed at the idea of waiting in line for a selfie with a celebrity, but I wanted this one. Our table was right by the door, and we were some of the first in line. I wanted to say some-thing. I didn't know what. I wanted her to know I'd felt seen by the show. I wanted her to see me.

"This is our first time out together as—as lesbians—and well, we knew if anywhere in Salt Lake would be a good place for it, it would be your show." It all came out in a jumbled breath, one that would surely be impossible to parse in the selfie assembly line.

Cameron looked at Kya and understood immediately. "Well, you look beautiful," she said warmly. We snapped a photo and hurried off, keeping the line moving. It's a terrible photo of me. I wanted to show it to everyone. But of course, I couldn't post it.

Years later, I wrote to her on Twitter. She had tweeted, "Younger queer/gnc folks are less willing to hate themselves than I was at their age and that will make all the difference." I replied, "Cameron, a little over two years ago my wife and I met you at a show in Salt Lake, it was her first time ever going somewhere presenting as a woman and we knew your show would be a safe place for that. It was such a lovely experience because you so clearly knew what it was like to grow up queer and religious and you were clearly keeping in mind what that kind of show meant in a red state. Anyways you probably don't remember meeting us but she came out to everyone this week and I just wanted you to know and thank you for being a step in our journey!"

To my surprise, she replied quickly. "I remember you two! Holy crap what a big week. Pls send my love. This is amazing."

Kya added, "Cameron, as the recently out wife in question, I just wanted to personally thank you as well. Being able to attend your show presenting as a woman was such a meaningful experience for me, and your genuine kindness at the meet & greet after is something I will always remember."

"Thank you for telling me this!" she responded again. "It was a real honor to witness your honesty that night xoxo"

Still riding the high of the Cameron Esposito show, I tried to find other moments to microdose honesty in the years before Kya could come out. The pandemic threw a wrench in our plans, making it harder to get electrolysis or find out how to do hormone replacement therapy, but making it much, much easier to grow her hair out and dress however she wanted at home. Nobody was just dropping by anymore.

My grad school cohort didn't quite know what to do about the pandemic either. We went home for spring break and were suddenly online until graduation. Someone organized a Zoom social, and it was chatty, still a novel experience. "Yeah, my wife and I ..." I said, and Kya glanced up in surprise from the couch. I saw some wheels spinning in my classmate's heads onscreen, but nobody asked questions.

"I was surprised to hear you say that," Kya confided in bed later.

"Well I just figured, none of them know you, and it's not like I'm going to see any of them again anyways."

"Oh yeah, that's what I figured, I'm not upset about it." A silence. "I liked it. Hearing you say it so casually, like it was an everyday thing."

––––––––––––––

Our move to Montana a few months later was abrupt. Spontaneous, to the point of maybe not being fully thought through. A few ward members halfheartedly showed up to help load our moving van, and the ministering sister I usually tried to avoid showed up as well. She was too elderly to help move, but she wanted our new address, to transfer our records — having clearly guessed our plan to move and fall off the map. I reluctantly gave it to her, but I had no intention of being moved *in* to our new apartment by the Mormons.

Instead, our moving van was met by the only two people I knew in Missoula: a pair of queer BYU alumni I'd never met in person.

I spent the pandemic quarantine watching a lot of Episcopal church on YouTube. The local reverend, a woman, seemed kind. "It's normal to have seasons where you wander," she preached in the homily, "And if you've been wandering for a time, we're happy you're here now."

I cried on the couch and imagined what I'd say if I showed up after the pandemic. "I don't know if I believe in God, but I want to, but I don't want to believe just because I want to, but I want to go to church. But I don't *want* a different church, I want *my* church. But they don't want me, and I like your church." I couldn't even think the words without crying too hard to speak. I wasn't going to cry like that in front of a stranger. I kept watching on YouTube.

––––––––––––––

"The Book of Mormon opens with the story of family that must flee Zion into the wilderness for its own safety," my friend Ted observed on Twitter. "That's what not going to church felt like for me." I had fled to Montana from Salt Lake. I had fled to Salt Lake from Provo. I had fled ... to Provo? I thought about it. I had fled to Provo.

Growing up, my dad had joked that as a kid his model of life was you finished high school, you served a mission, you got married, you graduated university, and then you died. The adults would laugh, and laugh, and my eleven-year-old forehead wrinkled in confusion. "It's funny because there's such a long time between graduating university and dying," my mom explained. I was unconvinced. There certainly didn't seem to be any steps after that, and that *was* the plan: you got married, you graduated from the University of Alberta, and then you died.

My dad drove me to a fireside on the very north end of Calgary. Some speaker from BYU, maybe worth the trip all the way across the city. We settled into the pews, me wearing my new black wedges from Le Chateau with the bow on them. The speaker passed out college packets—it wasn't a fireside at all, just a recruitment pitch. My dad never would have bothered with the drive if he'd have known.

I only had one uncle who had gone to BYU instead of an Alberta school, and he'd married an American and never moved back. But a conviction rose within me. This was what I was going to do: attend BYU, graduate unmarried, do a master's degree in Alberta, and *then* meet a nice boy, get married before I could become sinfully invested in a career, and my life would be over. "But what if you *do* meet an American?" my parents asked. I didn't know how to explain why I was so sure I'd graduate college unmarried. I didn't know why I was so sure.

Family legend held that at Thanksgiving during my uncle's Grade 12 year, the family had gone around the table to say what they were thankful for. "I'm thankful that next year I won't be here, because I'll be at BYU," he groused. My grandma had burst into tears and run from the room. I shifted eagerly in my seat at my own last Thanksgiving home, barely able to contain my grin, trying not to catch my mom's eye. I knew she knew the joke I was about to make, and I knew she wasn't going to be mad about it. "I'm thankful that next year I won't be here, because I'll be at BYU," I joked. Everyone laughed. I could tell my mom felt sad it was little bit true. I didn't know why it was a little bit true.

You graduate high school, you serve a mission, you get married, you graduate university. And then you die, with no goals left to conquer. I understood, in my cold Montana basement, why I had felt that strange, inexplicable urgency to go to BYU. I hadn't known why I couldn't go to the University of Alberta and meet a nice boy with a nice major that would land him a nice career with a nice house in the suburbs. I had just known that I couldn't, and I needed space to figure it out, and what better way to get space than to move to an entirely new country by yourself? And what better way to do that than to move to a nice, safe church school, to flee to Zion? Fleeing to Zion was in my blood—as Carol Lynn Pearson would say, my people were Mormon pioneers.

Of all the places for the answer to be "you're really queer." But where truth flies you follow.

I went to Zoë's school's Around the World Night alone. Kya stayed home with the baby. It was smarter, during this 23rd month of March 2020, to have a parent stay home with the unvaccinated baby, and if that parent happened to be the newly out trans woman who still didn't quite trust the liberalness of Missoula, well. She was Levi's favorite mom anyways.

I sat down with Zoë at her desk, and she waved excitedly to her "bestie." Her friend rushed over, trailed by not one, but two non-binary parents. My heart leaped, then fell again as I realized with chagrin that I'd automatically rolled out my "straightsona" for the school event. I tried my best to find a way to work in "my wife is at home with the baby."

"It did seem a little forced," Chance acknowledged later, "but in a good way. We were so excited too! They'd been best friends all year, and neither of them knew."

At Zoë's next birthday party, two of her friends were from queer families. We all sat at the table together as the science center's liquid nitrogen demonstration went on at the front of the room. "Okay, now a picture of the parents!" my mom said, Levi on her hip as she aimed her phone's camera. We smiled, and I wondered if my mom found the moment photo-worthy for the same reason I did. All us queer folks with the early-twenties conservative culture pregnancies, raising our children in community together.

Kya's updated passport finally came and, for the first time since Zoë was a baby, we made the trip back to Canada together. It was dark by the time we got to Lethbridge, and the winter drive from Lethbridge to Calgary felt like one I'd made countless times as a child. I looked out the window, searching for the Big Dipper out of habit, and realized with a shock that it nearly filled the sky this far north, seeming to touch the ground and scoop snow off the coulees. *It didn't seem oversized as a child*, I thought. *That was just the size it always was.*

The next day, we left Zoë at home with her grandpa while Kya, my mom and I went shopping together. Kya nervously bundled a scarf around her neck, not sure if her shave had been close enough.

"It's very safe here," my mom said. "I've seen like six trans women already."

"I know," I responded, "but she's still nervous."

We ate poutine and found some gorgeous outfits. I kept pulling out strappy party dresses for her to try on. "Not to buy, I just want to see you in them," I explained, and she rolled her eyes at me as I looked her up and down each time. We drove home along familiar roads, and I realized with a start that Calgary no longer felt solely Mormon to me. The church was still heavily present, of course, but it was a city of over a million people. I could live here, I realized. I could have a house, and send my kids to school, and go to work, and shop at Chinook Center, and Mormonism wouldn't weigh on me any more than it did in Missoula.

I started to wonder about pharmacy licensure in Alberta.

We arrived home to Chinese food from my favorite childhood restaurant. An uncle, an aunt, and my grandma came over, and I remembered that the last time I'd seen them—Kya still closeted—I'd said goodbye in my heart, just in case. My parents had assured us that everyone had taken the news of her being trans very well, but there was a difference between a theoretically good response and getting through dinner together incident-free.

It turned out to be just another dinner. The kind our extended family had always had, living only twenty minutes apart and always able to pop by. My aunt asked Kya about her job, and I admonished my cousin against playing with the butterfly knife too close to the baby. He stood up and joined the game of Apples to Apples instead, forming a team with Zoë and helping her read the words that were too big for her. All those years coming home by myself while Kya worked, wondering if next time we'd have to avoid extended family, and I'd never had to say goodbye at all.

We drove home that Sunday, in daylight that time, and I gripped the steering wheel through a winter storm as we drove past Okotoks, through Fort MacLeod, towards Chief Mountain and the border. Like a post-Christmas ski vacation to Montana, only I lived there and not here.

The wind swirled and danced on the icy highway. My mind wandered, and the bones of my ancestors buried under the prairies seemed to call out to me. *Come, join with us*, they beckoned. *Take your old place at the table. There is room enough, and to spare. Lie your head in the shadow of the mountains and sleep under the large northern stars.* I had packed my handcart with precious things, I had gathered my family and fled Zion into the wilderness, and somehow it had led me home.

ABOUT THE EDITOR

Kerry Spencer Pray teaches writing at Stevenson University in Owings Mills, Maryland. Mormon by birth, she taught at Brigham Young University for fourteen years and spent nearly twenty years in a mixed-orientation marriage. She lives with and coparents her two children with her wife and gay ex-husband, putting her nonnuclear family in the category of a polycule. You can follow her on X @swilua.